Prayer and Devotional Life of United Methodists

Prayer and Devotional Life of UNITED METHODISTS

*M*ETHODISTS

Steve **HARPER**

ABINGDON PRESS/Nashville

PRAYER AND DEVOTIONAL LIFE OF UNITED METHODISTS

Copyright © 1999 by Abingdon Press.

This book is printed on acid-free paper.

Scripture quotations are from the *Holy Bible: New Revised Standard Version*, copyright © 1990 Graded Press.

Library of Congress Cataloging-in-Publication Data

Harper, Steve.
    Prayer and devotional life of United Methodists / by Steve Harper.
        p.   cm.
    Includes bibliographical references.
    ISBN 0-687-08432-6 (alk. paper)
    1. Spiritual life--Methodist Church.   2. Methodist Church--Doctrines.
I. Title.
BX8349.H64H37   2000
248'.088'27--dc21   99-041013

99 00 01 02 03 04 05 06 07 08—10 9 8 7 6 5 4 3 2 1

MANUFACTURED IN THE UNITED STATES OF AMERICA

Contents

Chapter 1
This chapter examines the essence of prayer and devotional
life for United Methodists: holiness of heart and life. The
chapter is divided into two sections to enable this examination:
Communion (heart) and Compassion (life).

Chapter 2
Exploring these two central disciplines in Christian formation
and the Wesleyan Tradition guides readers into practical
expressions of what it means to read devotionally (lection divina) and pray continually (the life of prayer).

Chapter 3

Get Connected!
The idea of "connectionalism" is a significant part of our tradition. This chapter examines this idea from the two vantage
points of classic formation principles and the concrete structures Wesley used in early-Methodism, which still contain
applications for today.

Chapter 4

Go On!
The cultivation of prayer and devotional life in United
Methodism is not about "attainment" but rather about "journey." This chapter examines the pilgrimage motif through the
two lenses of the biblical doctrine of Christian perfection, and
the practical development of that message through an
action/reflection model of Christian formation.

Appendices

Introduction

IF I HAD written this book a year or two ago, it would have been different. It would have been informational and inspirational. I would have aimed to provide you with content to guide and motivate your prayer and devotional life. I still hope that will happen. But I am now writing for more. This is not only a book of information and inspiration, it is an *invitation*. A great movement of prayer is sweeping across the world today. There is no reason for a single United Methodist to be left out of what God is doing. I am inviting you to raise your sails and allow the "wind of the Spirit" to move you along in this crucial dimension of spiritual formation and Christian discipleship.

I am convinced that several hundred years from now, when the historians assess our age, one of the hallmarks they will note will be a world-wide revitalization of prayer and devotional life. A closer look at the Wesleyan tradition will reveal the same recovery. The period of time in which you and I are living will be seen as a period when world Methodism revived its commitment to personal and social holiness. And being true to that same tradition, the people called Methodist will be depicted as those who renewed their commitment to prayer, the chief means of grace in the Wesleyan tradition.

That is why information and inspiration alone will not suffice. You and I are being *invited* by the Spirit of God to step into the stream of spiritual renewal. God is using many means and media to issue this invitation, one of which is the witness within United Methodism itself. We do not have to step outside our tradition to find historic and contemporary evidence in support of the life of prayer and devotion. We are the recipients of a *living heritage*, one that can continue to transform us as we participate in it. I am writing this book as a "call to prayer," not just a volume about prayer.

The experience of writing this book has rekindled the flame of my own commitment to prayer and the devotional life. I have become a renewed seeker after the very thing I am asking you to consider. Together, we are fellow travelers on a journey God initiated long ago and has revived in our time. Let us pray that what has been true for others in times past will be made alive in us today.

Steve Harper

How to Use This Book

General Design

This book is designed for personal reading and small-group resourcing. It aims to provide increased knowledge about prayer and devotional life in our United Methodist Church. And, more important, it is intended to foster growth in the strengthening and actual practice of your devotional life. This book is part of a series produced to promote life-enriching practices for United Methodists.

The book has four chapters, with two sections in each chapter. It is hoped that you and your group will spend at least eight sessions in this study, giving attention to one of the sections at a time. This approach will maximize your exposure to the material and enrich your practice of the numerous suggestions contained in the text and also in the "Living It Out" segment at the end of each chapter. However, if you choose to do so, it is also possible to study this book in four sessions, giving attention to an entire chapter at each group meeting.

Regardless of the method and length of your study, pay special attention to the in-text applications and the "Living It Out" segment at the end of each chapter. The purpose of this book and the entire series is to help you move forward in your Christian life through concrete actions designed to deepen your faith and your life of discipleship. We need the information and inspiration of solid content, but it becomes stale material unless it finds expression in us.

The Initial Group Meeting

At this meeting, distribute the books and use the time for group members to get acquainted with each other and with the material to be studied. The following are suggestions for shaping this first meeting:

1. When the group has gathered, the group leader asks each person to introduce himself or herself. As each person does this, participants write the names in the front inside cover of the book. The list of names will become a prayer list. Participants covenant to pray for each other during their time together.

2. The leader asks the participants to form groups of three and take about five minutes to share responses to this statement: "In the past week, I felt closest to God when _____." The leader then calls the group back together and takes five to ten minutes to receive feedback from each of the triads, creating an overall sense of where, when, and how participants have felt near to God.

3. The leader asks the participants to open their books to the table of contents, to look at the basic content of the book, and then to skim through the pages. After about five minutes, the leader asks the participants to respond to the question, "What is most attractive to you in this book?" or to "What do you look forward to most in studying in this book?"

4. If the decision has not already been made, the group should determine how much time will be spent on this study. We encourage an eight-week period, using one of the sections in each chapter as the focus of each session. However, the group may choose a four-week study, covering an entire chapter at each session. Or, the group may wish to study the material in another way.

5. If the group is meeting at a time other than Sunday School, be sure to arrange to communicate the date, time, location, and length of each group meeting. This is especially important if they will rotate through more than one home during the course of the study. Participants need to have a clear understanding of where each group meeting will be held.
6. The leader should give the group an opportunity for any questions or additional comments and then turn to the Appendix and use the section entitled "Covenant Praying" as a way to conclude their time together.

Subsequent Meetings

1. If the group responds well to the exercise "When God was most near to me this past week," the leader may choose to continue it as a way of beginning each session.
2. The leader should divide the group into triads for five to ten minutes during which each person responds to the question, "What was the most important part of the study for you?" When the group reassembles, the leader asks each triad for these responses to see if there are any common points of interest. The leader may choose to use these responses as the basis for extended discussion.
3. Also, the leader should have the participants speak about their experiences of actual practice. What was most helpful? Why? Was anything not helpful? Why? Is there anything new? Did they discover anything they want to continue to practice?
4. The group should allow time for prayer. Appendix B provides suggestions for ways the group can pray together week after week.

5. The group should pray the "Covenant Prayer" together as a way of ending the session.

Other Possibilities
1. If a group is studying this book in the eight-week format, they may want to conclude their time with a mini-retreat. Appendix C provides a plan for a half-day retreat designed to bring closure to their experience with this material.
2. If the study has been especially fruitful, the group may want to go farther into the subject. Appendix E contains a list of available resources to help the study group do this personally and corporately.

Abbreviations

Certain texts are referred to often in the endnotes of this book. For easier reference, the following abbreviations are used:

BW *The Works of John Wesley* (Bi-Centennial Edition): a continuing series of volumes begun by Oxford University Press and now published by Abingdon Press. Under the chief editorship of Dr. Frank Baker, with the expertise of particular-volume editors, this series sets a new standard for Wesleyan scholarship. Whenever possible, primary references from Wesley are cited in this edition.

JW *The Works of John Wesley* (Jackson Edition): this fourteen-volume edition was published from 1829-31 by Thomas Jackson. It is the only complete edition of Wesley's Works in print, only gradually being replaced by the Bi-Centennial edition cited above.

TL *The Letters of John Wesley* (Telford Edition): this eight-volume edition was published in 1931 by Epworth Press in London. Until the Bi-Centennial Edition is finished, this is the most complete edition of Wesley's letters.

ENT *Explanatory Notes Upon the New Testament:* John Wesley published this one-volume work in 1755. It has been reprinted numerous times since.

EOT　　*Explanatory Notes Upon the Old Testament:* John Wesley published this three-volume work in 1765. It has gone in and out of print since that time.

Except for the Bi-Centennial Edition of Wesley's *Works*, which is moving forward under the auspices of Abingdon Press, the remaining sources cited above may or may not be in print at the time you are reading this book. Consult the latest edition of *Books in Print* to see if they are currently available.

Chapter 1

Living from the Heart

YEARS AGO, I attended a retreat led by Morton Kelsey. I looked forward to the time away with a person whose writings had helped shape my prayer and devotional life. I was not disappointed, even though I was surprised by the man himself. That can happen when you meet an author for the first time. He wore a T-shirt and carried the *Book of Common Prayer*. I was surprised by his simplicity on the one hand and his formality on the other. The retreat was a rhythmic variation between the two. In the most natural way, he led us to childlike innocence one moment and to classical insights the next.

I managed to sit next to him for one meal. He asked me the usual "get acquainted" questions. When I told him I was a professor of prayer and the spiritual life, he responded immediately and passionately, "You are in the most important work in the world. Over the years of my life, the number one question people have asked me is, "Can you help me with my prayer life?" Then by way of emphasis, he looked me squarely in the eye and repeated the words, "You are in the most important work in the world."

I will never forget that moment. And as I have continued to reflect on his words, I too have realized that the number one question I have been asked over the years is, "How can I grow in prayer and the devotional life?" It is the question I have asked myself repeatedly in my desire to grow as a Christian. The question arises naturally out of our being created in the image of God—a creation which places within us a divinely intended hunger for fellowship with the Almighty. At the same time, that hunger remains mysteriously insatiable. When we are at our best, we know there can be "something more." When we are at our worst, we swear there has to be "something else." We are correct at both extremes, and each new generation of Christians comes into the spiritual world asking for help in relation to prayer and the devotional life.

Susanna Wesley surely knew this as she cared for the spiritual well-being of her children. Along with her husband, Samuel, she was charged with the delicate but significant task of forming the spirits of each of her nineteen sons and daughters. She took nothing for granted, beginning to spend particular time with each of them before they could even speak. On repeated occasions, John Wesley testified that it was her influence which started and sustained him on his spiritual journey. Hers was an attention that combined the same qualities I noted in Morton Kelsey: simplicity on the one hand and formality on the other.

Two great dangers attend our quest for meaningful prayer and devotional life. The first is making it too easy. The second is making it too difficult. The first danger leads to the loss of reverence; the second, to the loss of motivation. Making our spiritual formation too easy caricatures it into superficiality. And if there is anything we don't need in the Christian world right now, it is shallow pietism. We have too many quick-fix formulas already. The challenge we face in our day is somehow to hear and heed the warning expressed

16

so well by Richard Foster: "Superficiality is the curse of our age. The doctrine of instant satisfaction is a primary spiritual problem. The desperate need today is not for a greater number of intelligent people, or gifted people, but for deep people."[1] This book is an invitation in that direction, an expression of our belief as Wesleyan Christians that prayer and devotional life is a means of grace to take us into the depth and richness of our faith.

The other extreme—making it too difficult—must likewise be avoided. Complexity counterfeits the spiritual life into something for super-saints. In every church I served as a pastor, I met people who were put off by some self-avowed "prayer warriors" who either didn't live consistently with their public praying or who made prayer seem like an exercise for the religious Olympians. We must also guard against turning prayer into a subject to be studied, a theology to be developed, and a language to be used on very limited and special occasions. This does not mean we ignore the legitimate difficulties associated with prayer and praying; it simply means we don't add to the difficulty by caricaturing prayer as something detached from ordinary people and everyday experiences.

When we move toward either extreme, our hearts tell us that truth and power lie elsewhere. That "elsewhere" is what I'm describing in this chapter as living from the heart. To seek for an improved prayer and devotional life "from the heart" is at the center of our Wesleyan tradition. John Wesley affirmed the classic creeds and confessions of the church. He was undoubtedly an orthodox Christian. But he knew that orthodoxy was not enough. Christianity written down, read, and recited on worshipful occasions could never capture the totality of the faith. The core of Christian faith was, and still is, a life-giving relationship with Jesus Christ, a quality and depth of religious commitment that Wesley repeatedly referred to as "heart religion."[2] Likewise, living from the heart must be the starting point and energizing center for a meaningful and sustained life of prayer and devotion today.

Failure to root ourselves here makes us subject to all sorts of inadequate substitutes. I mention two only to illustrate. The first is equating prayer and devotional life with particular systems, plans, and programs. Working the system can become the end, rather than a means to the end (i.e., "heart religion"). When this happens, we fall prey to a quantification of the spiritual life that puts the emphasis on what we do, how much we do, how often we do it, and how we operate during our times of prayer and devotion. This substitute becomes even worse when we add the tendency to see our way of prayer and devotion as "the" one tried and true way, casting judgment on those who may relate to God differently than we do.

The second inadequate substitute relates more to attitude than to action. It is the notion that we are somehow *obligated* to pray and have a regular devotional life. I call it "hortatory spirituality"—the widespread (often legalistic) application of all sorts of oughts, shoulds, and musts in relation to our faith formation. This substitute becomes even worse when we suppose these come from God, viewing God as the main one who "lays it on us." I have lost count of the number of people who have told me that they gave up on prayer and the devotional life because it was so loaded down with heavy expectations.

The first substitute falsifies prayer and the devotional life by roughly equating it with methods and practices. The second counterfeits it by making it appear to be a legalistic activity aimed to hold back God's disappointment with us. The first approach leads to performance anxiety; the second to perfectionism. Both are foreign to the spirit we want to cultivate through the use of this book, and, more important, through our development as Christian disciples.

18

Instead, we want to cultivate prayer and devotional life as "living from the heart." But what does this mean? Without some notion of an answer, we are no closer to vital prayer and devotional life. We are introduced to a hollow concept. However, with some idea of what this means, we are at a place for taking first steps in prayer and the devotional life (if we are new Christians) or renewing our spiritual formation (if we have been Christian for some time). In fact, the idea of living from the heart is much more than an idea, it is a God-created energy which draws us to God as surely as iron filings are drawn to a magnet.

The concept of living from the heart goes all the way back to the early church. By about 300 A.D., the Christian community was experiencing intense pressure to conform to the ways of the world. Believers were seeking means to resist this temptation and remain faithful to God. The experience of Abba Arsenius illustrates the dilemma many were facing. Arsenius was a Roman senator who lived at the court of Emperor Theodosius, serving as a tutor to the emperor's two sons. Surrounded by ornate privilege and ostentatious prosperity, Arsenius could feel the eroding effects in his soul. He prayed, "Lord, lead me in the way of salvation." From deep within he heard the words, "Arsenius, flee from the world and you will be saved." Honoring this impression, he sailed secretly from Rome to Alexandria.

It was not long before he realized that a mere change of location did not alleviate his problems. He prayed again, "Lord, lead me in the way of salvation." The answer came back in a similar but expanded version: "Arsenius, flee, be silent, pray always, for these are the sources of sinlessness."[3] The three words—flee, be silent, and pray—summarize what came to be the notion of living from the heart. In the history of Christian spirituality, they have become a window through which one can see the journey of the soul. They characterize the disposition of one in search of a dynamic and deepening relationship with God.

You may wonder why an ancient story like this would have any place in a contemporary call to United Methodists to recover a revitalized prayer and devotional life. The answer lies in John Wesley himself and the strategic elements he included in the early Methodist movement. With respect to the notion of fleeing, the entry requirement for membership in the United Societies was "a desire to flee the wrath to come."[4] Wesley knew that people can be heading toward God only when they have determined to be moving away from anything and everything destructive to abundant life.

We do not make the journey toward God unless and until we are convinced that where we are is the wrong place. Fleeing is not psychological escapism; rather, it is the recognition that life apart from a transforming experience with God through Jesus Christ is artificial life—dangerous life. Thus, to have been awakened (by God's prevenient grace) to a desire to "flee" is the starting point for subsequent spiritual formation. It continues to be a motivation for subsequent growth in grace as we refrain from that which is destructive to ourselves or to others. The early Methodist movement was rooted in a commitment to do no harm—that is, to flee from entertaining or participating in anything that intentionally injures another.[5] Our Wesleyan tradition is rooted in the early church's understanding of the significance of this first step in the spiritual life.

At the same time, Wesley knew from his own experience that growth in grace must ultimately be based upon and fueled by that which is positive. It is not enough to concentrate on what we are leaving behind or to speak of what we don't do anymore. Even if we are delivered from great sin and frustration, we must eventually shift our focus to the results of our deliverance. So, members of the United Societies were encouraged to do all the good they could.[6]

The foundation of their spiritual formation was the calculated and continuous practice of righteousness. This blend between abandoning everything negative and embracing everything positive fueled the personal and corporate life of early Methodism.

This view of the Christian life puts us into the mainstream of Christian spiritual life and development. Living from the heart creates the context for growth, enabling us to see the need to cultivate the twin virtues of authentic discipleship: communion and compassion. These qualities are the core of the Wesleyan tradition with its twofold emphasis on personal and social holiness. Personal holiness roots us deeply in communion with God. Social holiness instills compassion within us. Together, they motivate and enable us to live vocationally in Jesus' name. The rest of this chapter will concentrate on these two central features of living from the heart.

Communion

It is an amazing thing to discover that what God wants most from us—is *us*! God surely wants to work in us and through us, but prior to that (and deeper than that) is God's desire to relate to us—to have fellowship with us. In the mid-1960's, I had an experience that shaped the way I continue to view my life as a disciple. I was a young Christian, still caught up in the wonder of my newfound faith and beginning to consider how I might live my life for God. There were several people whom I admired for their faith and their commitment to God, and in some ways I was trying to be like them—attempting to take qualities from them and incorporate those into my life. In and of itself that desire was not bad, but it had the potential to deflect me from the deeper reality of being a follower of Christ.

I was walking down the street, passing by the post office as I went along. The Vietnam war was in full swing, and there was an Army recruitment poster standing on the sidewalk. Uncle Sam pointed his bony finger at me, and the caption underneath the picture read, "I want you." I knew it was an invitation to join the military, but at the same moment, I heard it as God's word for me: "Steve, I want *you*. I don't want you to be a copy of anyone else. I want *you*."

The words burned into my soul, and I received them as God's desire for me. For nearly forty years I have continued to learn what this means and have struggled often to make it real. I have likewise met many people who find it almost unbelievable to think that God wants *them*, rather than a warmed-over version of someone else. Prayer and the devotional life rests on this unshakable fact: God wants us!

We carry around with us a continual reminder that it is so. Most of us learned about it in elementary school. Our teacher said, "Look at your hands." We put our hands out in front of us as he or she continued the amazing story: "On the end of each finger are little lines called fingerprints. Look carefully; the lines on one finger are different from the lines on any of the others." We stared at our hands and sure enough, it was true! But there was more as our teacher told us to compare the lines on our hands with the fingerprints of the person sitting next to us. They were different! But the most amazing reality was yet to come as our teacher told us, "No one else has your fingerprints. No one who has ever lived, no one who is now living, or anyone who will live someday will ever have your fingerprints. Your fingerprints make you absolutely unique."

Our fingerprints are a tangible reminder of our individuality and our unrepeatable value in the sight of God. It makes no sense to believe that God takes the time to etch into the ends of our fingers little lines which differentiate us from everyone else and then turns around and mass produces human souls. Rather, our fingerprints are divinely created evidence that we are a distinct and prized self, made in the image of God.

We are never more "ourselves" before God than when we pray, because when we pray, we bring nothing else with us. We are not "doing" anything at the moment, but paradoxically, we are doing the most important thing—we are giving God our *selves*. We are symbolically holding up our hands, asking God to relate to us with the specific attention our "soul print" deserves. An ancient proverb says, "God looks for us often, but most of the time we are not at home." Prayer is being "at home" with God—spirit to Spirit, life to Life. Prayer is discovering that the God who made us wants to receive us and relate to us. These deep moments of intimacy and fellowship provide the sinews of the faith which inevitably compels us to go into the world to act in Jesus' name.

Prayer is exercising the muscle of the soul, so it can enable us to live for God. Prayer propels us into the world precisely because we know that the God who "wants us" is the God who "wants everyone." Prayer is not an exhibition of selfishness, but rather the energy of servanthood. The specificity of our soul-print relationship does not isolate us from others or insulate us from sensitivity to their needs. Rather, prayer reveals the loving heart of God for humankind and the broken heart of God for any persons who are failing to be the unique, unrepeatable selves God intended them to be. Prayer shows us that the basis of redemption is God's unwillingness to accept caricatures and counterfeits. Prayer reveals God's love for the whole world through the coming of Christ, and we are invited in the prayer relationship to become disciples of Christ in the service of others.

Unfortunately, some people have missed this, choosing to misrepresent prayer as "wasted time" when we ought to be "out there doing something." The failure of this view lies precisely in our forgetting that working for God is preceded by walking with God. Furthermore, prayer makes it plain that what God calls us to do is *impossible* apart from a prior attaining of God's perspective and a personal anointing with God's power.

Communion with God in prayer prevents the soul-draining experience of religious humanism. Long ago, the prophet Zechariah declared the inescapable principle that it is "not by might, nor by power, but by my spirit, says the LORD of hosts" (4:6). Living from the heart is living with a profound and perpetual remembrance that prior to any act of servanthood lies God's desire to enter into transforming fellowship with us. As we noted earlier, we are made in the image of God, and that design enables communion to take place.

As we view our Christian life this way, we are dealing with the Wesleyan emphasis upon experience. John Wesley was not content (either for himself or the early Methodists) to leave religion as something purely objective, rational, and cognitive. To be sure, he was an orthodox Christian. But he knew there could be "dead orthodoxy"a view of Christianity that had all the form but none of the life. And yet, Christ himself had said, "I came that they may have life, and have it abundantly" (John 10:10). Wesley could not be content with any expression of Christianity that omitted a deeply personal and profoundly meaningful experience. He sought for every believer what he strove for himself: to be a full participant in God's drama of salvation, not merely a detached observer of it.[7]

This same spirit is seen in Jacob Albright, a spiritual forefather of The United Methodist Church. Born in 1759 in Montgomery County, Pennsylvania, he began his journey in the Lutheran Church. After serving in the Revolutionary War, he settled on a farm in Lancaster County, Pennsylvania.

After his conversion, he was strongly attracted to the spiritual atmosphere of the Methodist class meeting. As his commitment to Christ deepened, he was known for his long periods of communion with God, especially using prayer and fasting as his central means of grace.[8] Out of these times alone with God, Albright discovered the substance and power of his spiritual life.

In the twentieth century, Dr. Frank Laubach expressed the connection between experience and a deep devotional life. He began each day with this prayer, "God, what are you doing in the world today that I can help you with?" His prayer teaches at least three profound things about communion. First, our communion with God is rooted in God's prior and ongoing activity. We do not get there first. When we awaken to a new day, God is already at work; indeed, God is constantly at work. If this were not true, even for a millisecond, the whole creation would collapse into nothingness. Thus when we commune with God, we are in the presence of the unceasingly active and faithful God.

Second, our communion does not throw us into a feverish and futile attempt to do everything. Rather we ask for that portion of God's work which God designs for us to be involved in. We recognize there are innumerable aspects of that work which we are not to take on. This is prayer that both engages us and protects us. It is prayer that makes us healthy servants of God, not frenetically driven ones! Our communion is rooted in our desire to offer ourselves in service to God. But it is also the recognition that our service will be limited and focused. Prayer and devotional life thus become experiences of reality, not fantasy. In a similar way, E. Stanley Jones referred to his morning prayer times as "going to the listening post." And out of those moments of devoted listening, he received his "marching orders" for the day.

Third, Laubach's prayer illustrates the spirit of true communion: our desire to do God's will. We want to see what

God is doing in the world today, discover our part in it, and submit ourselves to that portion of it. Without this, our communion can become self-centered and self-serving. But prayer and devotional life in the Wesleyan tradition is no "me and Jesus" kind of thing. It is a communing with God in the deepest levels of our souls, so that our lives become truly and completely devoted to Christ, and that they come to be instruments through which God can work.

Christ himself exemplified this kind of communion when he told his disciples, "I do nothing on my own, but I speak these things as the Father instructed me. And the one who sent me is with me; he has not left me alone, for I always do what is pleasing to him" (John 8:28-29). Where did Jesus discern what to do and what to say? Where did he receive these instructions from his Father? He did so during his times of deep and sustained prayer—communion at its truest and best.

To see this eliminates once and for all the mistaken notion that deep and sustained periods of communion with God create life avoidance. To be sure there is a temptation to move that way—to define and evaluate our spirituality exclusively in relation to the intake moments of our spiritual formation. But genuine communion as exemplified by Jesus and witnessed to by the saints of the ages will take us in an entirely different direction.

If this vision of communion is as genuine and life-giving as we believe it to be, we must now turn our attention to some ways of establishing it in our lives. This book is invitational, not merely informational. It is conceived with the intention of providing concrete and practical ways to turn theories into practices. From here on, we will integrate ideas about prayer and devotional life with specific counsel aimed to help us participate in and experience what we are describing. After all, this book is part of a series aimed to promote life-enriching practices. Communion is cultivated through more ways and means than we can describe in a book of this nature and length, but the following expressions are surely representative of life lived from the heart in fellowship with God.

First, honestly assess your commitment to love God and your neighbor. Communion makes sense and occurs only as the outflow of a life devoted to God and committed to Christ. Jesus' lifting up of the two great commandments is the starting point for the kind of prayer and devotional life we are commending. John Wesley warned against every form of spiritual delusion. He differentiated between being an "almost Christian" and being an "altogether Christian."[9] As you make this evaluation, be sure to avoid any legalistic notions. Rather, make the assessment in relation to how your commitment fosters a desire to spend time with God. You may discover that previous experiences or currently held notions actually reduce your motivation for communion. Frame your examination in relation to the goal of deepening your relationship with God. It is not too much to ask you to stop right where you are and pray a prayer in words like these: "God, I want to have a prayer and devotional life that brings me close to you—one that enables me to cherish your presence and receive your counsel. I commit my life anew to you in this moment. I seek your face, and I invite you to dwell in me totally and continually. In Jesus' name, Amen."

Second, this kind of consecration will create a hunger for growth in prayer and the devotional life. Such hunger is fostered by ongoing periods of silence and solitude. Find times and places where you can be alone with God. The busyness which so easily consumes us will make this action challenging in and of itself, but there is no other way. The frenetic pace of contemporary living leaves us feeling strung out, resentful, and empty. The Bible tells us that Jesus regularly withdrew to quiet and deserted places to pray (Luke 5:15-16). If the Son of God needed these times of deliberate separation from the rat race, how can we imagine to grow in prayer and devotional life without them?

Third, use such quiet times both to listen and to learn. Bombarded by words in the world today, we easily think communion with God is about speaking. Because prayer is so often connected to speaking, we naturally think that our words need to show up early and often in the devotional life. But the witness of believers for twenty centuries is that communion is more about listening. We will have more to say about this as we move along in this book, but it is important to nail it down at this point. Communion is rooted in receptivity, to the cultivation of a devotional style that seeks to be addressed by God. A study of the lives of previous believers reveals that they spent protracted periods in wordless prayer. Such prayer was not "mindless," but rather was an exercise in considering God's will and way instead of reporting ours. Such listening has always been rooted in Scripture and in other substantive material. It is not a free-flowing experience of subjectivism. It is more a disposition of the heart than a specific methodology. It is a practice based on the belief that we are made to "hear from" God (imago dei), and that if we are patient and persistent, we will. It is the conviction that God's word is primary and our words are secondary.

Early in my pastoral ministry, I had an experience which anchored this conviction in my life. One day, at the close of my quiet time, I discovered that I didn't have anything on my prayer list to pray for. That tells you something about the limits of my praying back then, but it is not the point I want to make. As I approached my usual moment of intercession, I realized that nothing came to mind. Jeannie and I were on good terms. Our children were healthy. No one in the congregation was in the hospital. The church was relatively problem free. So, I made an attempt to wrap things up and move into my day. But I was stopped cold by an inward impression of God's Spirit that went like this: "Steve, there may be some days when you don't have anything particularly important to say to me, but there is never a day when I do not have something significant to say to you." In that moment I learned at a completely new level the necessity of listening—an insight that has stayed with me ever since that day. We are called to practice periods of silent receptivity and to act in relation to what we hear.

Fourth, if you feel a strong attraction to communion, turn to the Appendix for additional resources to take you farther in this dimension of prayer and devotional life. Also consider having a conversation with a friend to see how he or she cultivates communion with God. Interaction with others roots our desire to grow in real-life experiences, connecting us with what others have actually done. In fact, most of what we incorporate into our spiritual growth is given to us through the testimony or example of someone else. This fact necessitates a word about community.

We are so prone today to individualism and isolationism (cocooning) that we can fail to remember that the kind of communion we are describing is never divorced from interaction with others. Pope John Paul II has captured the right perspective by saying, "It is not even thinkable that a Christian should live solely for himself."[10] When John Wesley conceived of the people later called Methodist, he resolutely rejected all ideas and structures which would generate or reinforce independent and disconnected discipleship. He had seen the damage which isolationism and quietism produced. Methodism as a reflection of genuine Christianity has always been faith in community. It is no accident that communion and community flow from the same root. Authentic and vital prayer and devotional life will always include a corporate dimension. We will revisit this theme as we move along.

Compassion

Genuine communion with God enables us to know and share God's heart. Compassion is the natural outflow of a vital devotional life. As Wesleyan Christians, we stand in the historic holiness tradition. Personal holiness (here described as communion) fosters and strengthens social holiness (compassion). The two are as inseparable as inhaling and exhaling. At any given moment, we may be doing one of them, but the other will not be far behind. If we only inhale, we will explode. If we only exhale, we will be exhausted. If we only commune with God, we will become "spiritually bloated"; if we only exhale, we will become "spiritually depleted." Spiritual breathing (authentic prayer and devotional life) includes a natural rhythm between communion and compassion.

John and Charles Wesley were hardly a year beyond their heart-warming experiences with God before they ran into those who tried to convince them that personal holiness was all they needed. Groups known as "quietists" urged people to cease from all outward actions and wholly withdraw from the world. They emphasized communion without compassion. After examining their claims, John Wesley concluded that quietism was false Christianity—directly opposite to the gospel of Christ. He wrote, "The gospel of Christ knows of no religion but social, no holiness but social holiness. 'Faith working by love' is the length and breadth and depth and height of Christian perfection."[11]

Communion is the means by which we establish and maintain our relationship with God. It is the way we receive from God. But when this dimension of the spiritual life is activated in us, it cannot be contained within us. Dr. Theodore Runyon describes the necessary outflow by writing, "What is received demands further expression; that is its nature. If what comes to us is God's loving, though not uncritical, affirmation, this affirmation cannot be hoarded but must be shared. The love *to* us from the world's Savior flows *through* us to all the world's creatures, especially those in need and distress."[12] Another statement from Wesley further grounds this conviction in our heritage, "True Christianity cannot exist without both the inward experience and outward practice of justice, mercy, and truth."[13]

Without realizing it, we are the heirs of an unfortunate bifurcation. More than a century ago, some of our predecessors in the faith began to differentiate between the "personal gospel" and "the social gospel." Depending on which camp a particular adherent was in, that part of the gospel was deemed preferable to the other. The result was a separation of spiritual dynamics that our United Methodist heritage has sought to hold together. If we are to recover a genuine Wesleyan spirituality, we must strive to hold communion and compassion together. In one moment of time, God may call us to the one; at a later moment, the other. To use the statement from the wedding ceremony, "We must not separate what God has joined together."

The word *compassion* is derived from the Latin words *pati* and *cum*, which combine to mean, "to suffer with." Compassion calls us to be "with" people, especially those in need. It is that part of the spiritual life which takes us outside ourselves and brings us into caring relationships with others. Compassion begins in the heart of God, in the nature of the One who has chosen to be with us. The creation stories in Genesis reveal a God who walks and talks with Adam and Eve, even providing for them after their rebellion. The deliverance stories in Exodus portray a God who sees the affliction of people and comes to their rescue. The climax of God's compassion (i.e., God's being "with" us) is the Incarnation—as Jesus, the Word made flesh, dwells among us (John 1:14). Jesus is Emmanuel, *God with us.*

Compassion also means that God is *active* among us. It is possible to be with someone without doing them much good. This is not Christian compassion, nor is it the compassion of God, which illustrates and empowers our compassion. God comes to be with us as the One who can deliver us from evil. The compassionate God wipes away our tears (Isaiah 25:8), binds up our broken hearts (Isaiah 61:1), and welcomes us home when we wander far away (Luke 15:11-24). David could hardly find words adequate to describe the compassionate God when he wrote Psalm 103:1-5:

> Bless the Lord, O my soul,
>   and all that is within me,
>   bless his holy name.
> Bless the Lord, O my soul,
>   and do not forget all his benefits—
> who forgives all your iniquity,
>   who heals all your diseases,
>   who redeems your life from the Pit,
>   who crowns you with steadfast love and mercy,
>   who satisfies you with good as long as you live
>   so that your youth is renewed like the eagle's.

The compassionate God is not merely with us, but is also in our presence as one who is active among us, taking the form of a servant and providing us with all that we need for life. But there is more! Compassion is an expression of obedience—of fidelity to God's own nature. Karl Barth wrote, "It belongs to the inner life of God that there should take place within it obedience."[14] This means that compassion is not an obligation which God has to provide, but an act of mercy which flows from a heart of divine love.

Our compassion is related to and reflective of God's compassion. As we commune with God, we feel God's heart and hear God's call to be "with" people—yet, not merely with them but also with them through acts of service. And as our communion with God matures our life of faith, we find that compassion is not a duty imposed upon us, but rather a desire welling up from within us. The compassionate God creates within us a compassionate life, which becomes a compassionate way.[15]

At this point, you may be ready to ask, "What does this have to do with the prayer and devotional life of United Methodists?" We know that the way of compassion is the way of Christ and his disciples. But how is this truth transferred into our tradition? The answer emerges from an examination of "the means of grace" in the Wesleyan tradition. Communion and compassion are joined into a dynamic devotional life through the means of grace.[16]

Prayer and devotional life is essentially a participation in the mind, heart, and work of Jesus Christ, made possible by his indwelling presence within us. It follows that such participation must have ways of transferring grace from God's heart to ours. The electrical current of God's heart must flow through some kind of "wiring" into our hearts. In the Wesleyan tradition, this transfer has been called "the means of grace." John Wesley defined the means of grace as "the ordinary channels of conveying his grace into the souls of men."[17] He believed that if we are to have a heart renewed after the image of God, there must be means to achieve that end.

He divided the means of grace into two groups: instituted and prudential. The instituted means of grace roughly corresponded to the Roman Catholic idea of works of piety. The prudential means of grace roughly approximated the Roman Catholic notion of works of mercy.[18] With respect to the Wesleyan tradition, the instituted means of grace more directly advanced personal holiness; the prudential means gave expression to social holiness. With respect to this book, the instituted means of grace more nearly correspond to what we have said about communion, while the prudential means of grace more closely foster the compassion we have been describing. Yet, it is important to note that the instituted and prudential means of grace were never "separated." They operated as another expression of the inhaling and exhaling necessary for authentic spirituality.

The instituted means of grace include prayer, searching the Scriptures, the Lord's Supper, fasting, and Christian conference. The prudential means of grace gave counsel to avoid all harm, to do as much good as possible, and to attend the ordinances of God. If this is your first time to study the means of grace in our Wesleyan tradition, a brief summary may be helpful.

With respect to the instituted means of grace, prayer creates and sustains the primary relationship between ourselves and God. Wesley called prayer "the chief means" of grace. The Christian faith is essentially a relationship. Relationships are created and sustained by good communication. Prayer is God's gift of communication—God's way of establishing primary dialog between us. Furthermore, grace precedes our response to it. Therefore (as Wesley put it), if we desire the grace of God to be at work in us, we must wait for it in prayer. Prayer is the means of *receiving*. Wesley used the comparison to Jesus' words of asking, seeking, and knocking—calling prayer the way of finding the pearl of great price—God's grace—the means of entering into the Kingdom.

John Wesley's own example is one of devoted and sustained prayer across the years of his life. Before he could read or talk, his parents taught him to make religious gestures. As soon as he was able, he was taught the Lord's prayer. He moved on to utilize the prayer system provided by *The Book of Common Prayer*. He incorporated spontaneous prayers into his devotions. He prayed privately and with others. He prayed when he was on top of the world and also when he was in the depths of despair. In all these ways he was strengthening his relationship with God.

Searching the scriptures calls us to more than random or superficial Bible reading. It is a close and systematic study of God's Word, giving attention to both the Old and New Testaments. Wesley believed practicing this means of grace "confirms and increases true wisdom" as we come in contact with divine revelation.[19] For the most part, he used the lectionary texts in *The Book of Common Prayer* for his selection of daily reading. But he used other patterns as well during the course of his lifetime. And as he read, he mingled prayer throughout the process. In contemporary United Methodism, the *Disciple Bible Study* experience is an illustration of the Wesleyan principle of searching the Scriptures.

The Lord's Supper was a mainstay in the devotional life of early Methodists. Growing as they did out of the Anglo-Catholic tradition, the Eucharist was a sacrificial meal which afforded communicants the opportunity to meet the risen Christ. In Wesley's day, holy communion had lost much of its influence. People partook rarely. It is not too much to say that the Methodist movement was a sacramental revival as well as an evangelical one. Through preaching and singing, the Wesleys called their followers back to a regular participation at the Lord's table. And more, they urged the observance of the sacrament to create a spirit of "constant communion" in those who received it. In the past decade, we have seen evidences of a much-needed sacramental revival in our denomination. We are recovering the connection of Word and Table, which shaped the worship of the early church and flowed so powerfully into and through the Wesleyan tradition.

Fasting provided a means to redeem time and give more concentrated attention to the things of God. The point of fasting was not its intensity or its duration. Rather, it was a devotional act which enabled one to give time to God which normally was given to eating. Wesley's custom was to begin his fast after dinner on Thursday and continue it until mid-afternoon on Friday. His practice followed the pattern of Christ's passion, beginning with his prayer in the Garden of Gethsemani until the hour of his death on the cross. Fasting was also Wesley's initial preparation to receive the Lord's Supper in church on Sunday. By focusing his attention on God through fasting, he felt he would be better able to receive the grace of God which would be offered him in the sacrament.

Christian conference is a term Wesley used to describe various forms of conversation, covenant life, and sharing which brought Christians into contact with each other. Under its umbrella we can see routine "religious talk" (as Wesley called it in his diary), spiritual direction, small-group sharing, and the more structural aspects of early Methodism: the societies, classes, bands, and annual conferences. Wesley believed that God bestows grace upon believers when they are willing to "confer" with one another. There is collective wisdom given when dedicated disciples converse and fellowship with one another.

Before we turn our attention to the prudential means of grace, let us recognize that the instituted means of grace are part of the formation of compassion. They are the link between communion and the compassion which is to flow from it. They dispose the heart to receive God's grace and transmit it to others. They help to create the mind of Christ and to stir the will to act accordingly. Each of the five instituted means served the dual purpose of strengthening the practitioner and also shaping him or her into faithful servants of Jesus Christ.

The three prudential means of grace come into the picture to guide us in the concrete acts of charity and caregiving which constitute the compassionate life.[20] The first exhortation to "do no harm" echoes all the way back to the ethics of the Hippocratic oath, reminding believers that their first act of compassion is to be sure they are not causing damage or suffering to others. This kind of conscious avoidance is quickly followed by its positive counterpart: "do good." Christian compassion is known not only by what we do *not* do to others, but more especially by what we actually *do* for their welfare.

The third prudential means was "attending upon all the ordinances of God." The ordinances of God were simply the five instituted means of grace in their corporate expression. By calling the early Methodists to this kind of life in Christ, Wesley was tying the instituted and prudential means of grace together, and he was further strengthening the conviction that both communion and compassion are formed and increased in community.

Once again, we are at a point where we must take these facts and principles and translate them into practical expressions. Surely the first and most obvious aspect is our embrace and practice of the means of grace. In terms of devotional practice, the use of the means of grace is at the heart of Wesleyan spirituality. As you move through the days of your life, consciously practice the instituted and prudential means of grace.

Second, include in your praying this specific request, "God, show me where you want me to express your compassion to others." Keep praying this prayer until you begin to get a concrete sense of tangible actions the Spirit of God is inviting you to take. As you expand your consciousness with respect to compassion, keep three areas in mind: (1) near-at-hand ways to be personally involved, (2) farther-away opportunities you can be part of occasionally, and (3) opportunities to help others through your charitable giving. Ask God to strengthen your compassionate heart in relation to each of these areas.

Third, if you subscribe to a newspaper, read it with an eye toward intercessory prayer for the people and needs you see there day after day. You can do the same as you listen to the radio or watch television. These media are excellent resources to call us to prayer in relation to real-life situations.

Fourth, familiarize yourself with community-service ministries. Some may be carried out right in your local church. Others may be free-standing organizations in your city. Select two or three. Call them and ask for information. Find out when their basic ministries are carried out and stop by to see for yourself what is being done. As you do this, prayerfully consider if God is inviting you to become involved in some way.

Fifth, ask others how they establish and maintain a compassionate spirit. In our age when individualism is so prevalent, we must exert our wills to live outside of ourselves. Often we can get help and receive clues when we ask others to tell us what they do to live for others.

Sixth, if compassion holds a strong draw for you, consult the Appendix for additional resources to further your knowledge and growth in this area. Find out from others what resources they have found useful in deepening their compassion.

A word of caution is in order as we conclude this section on compassion. If you have a particularly sensitive spirit, you can easily become overwhelmed by the enormous need for compassion in our world today. And it is a short step from feeling overwhelmed to believing that what you do makes little difference. Beware this lie, and hold on to the fact that every act of kindness has significance. Moreover, do not look far away for places where compassion is called for. Look close at hand. Occupy your time with acts of compassion to those nearest and dearest to you, even as you remain open to God's guidance regarding other more-distant opportunities. There are more than five billion people on the earth today. Imagine the enormous good that would be done if each of us gave faithful attention to the people and situations that are a part of our everyday living. A global network of compassion would be instantly and continuously formed through the multiplied billions of actions done in the name and spirit of Jesus. So, give yourself to the things you can do—and do what you can for Christ.

Living from the heart is a contemporary way to express the essence of prayer and devotional life in the Wesleyan tradition. It connects us with the stream of Christian history where godly women and men have given themselves repeatedly to the communion and compassion we have described. Living from the heart roots us in a classic theology of grace as we seek God's perspectives for living and God's power to live in relation to those perspectives. Living from the heart enables us to practice our devotional life with personal authenticity and in relation to the concrete realities we face. Most especially, living from the heart enables us to participate in and to fulfill Wesley's exhortation to "stir up the spark of grace that is in you, and [God] will give you more grace."[21]

Living It Out

In addition to the in-text guidance given throughout the book, this segment will conclude each chapter. Do not feel that you have to practice every suggestion made. Some are given to help you ponder what you have read; others are offered to improve your practice of a particular aspect of prayer and devotional life. Use the ones which best enable you to incorporate what you have read. At the same time, use this segment as a way to consider new ideas and to try new things.

1. Where in your experience has your prayer and devotional life been too easy (leading to superficiality), and where has it been too difficult (leading to complexity)? How did the chapter help you find another alternative?

2. What do the words "flee, be silent, and pray" mean to you at this time in your life? Is one word more significant for you than another? Why? What is one concrete action you could attach to each word to make it applicable to your life right now?

3. Take Frank Laubach's morning prayer (page 25) and pray it yourself for a week. Keep paper at hand to record the insights which come to you as you pray this prayer at the beginning of your day.

4. Review the five instituted means of grace. Rank them in the order of their current relevance in your devotional life. Look at the one which is least active or influential. Consider one concrete way to practice this means of grace, and do it for the next two weeks. Again, record your insights.

5. Do the same with the three prudential means of grace. Take the one that is least active in your life and develop a plan to live it out for the next two weeks. Record your insights.

6. Assess your compassion in relation to the three levels mentioned on pages 36-37. Can you identify an actual involvement in each of the levels? If not, begin to prayerfully consider how you can become active in the levels which are lacking in your life. You may want to pay special attention at the next group meeting to see how others are living the compassionate life in these areas.

7. None of us can do everything at once. Before you leave this chapter, is there an aspect of communion or compassion you want to implement sometime in the future? If so, name it. And, more important, commit to a time when you will revisit that element and seek for ways to make it an active part of your prayer and devotional life. (Note: This final question is one you can use with each of the remaining chapters to help provide continuity and follow-through to your experience.)

Chapter 2

Read and Pray Daily

GOD DOES NOT call us to have a devotional time; God calls us to live a devotional life. The communion and compassion we examined in the last chapter are not meant to be an occasional experience, but rather a continual expression of our love for God and others. Using the instituted and prudential means of grace is not intended to be an on-again, off-again thing. The means of grace are designed to create a spirit of devotion which anoints and attends us throughout the day. Living from the heart expresses a spiritual formation which cannot be segmented or separated from all other aspects of our lives. Every moment is a God-moment, charged with the possibility of encounter and involvement. Prayer and devotional life in the Wesleyan tradition cannot and must not be viewed in any other way.

At the same time, living from the heart calls for our participation in concrete acts of devotion which nourish our souls. It sounds pious for someone to say, "I don't take time for devotions, I just live in the presence of God all day long." But it doesn't work that way! After studying the lives of the saints for more than thirty years, I have never found a single disciple of Jesus who failed to include stated periods and acts of formation in the midst of a total life devoted to God. In the same way that we pause in the course of the day for specific meals, we likewise practice the presence of God through fixed moments of devotion. Without these definite acts, the soul withers just as the body would if we did not take time to eat.

One of the early Methodist preachers was "withering." He wrote to John Wesley about it, and Wesley's response has become a classic quote in our tradition: "O begin! Fix some part of every day for private exercises. You may acquire the taste which you have not: what is tedious at first will afterward be pleasant. Whether you like it or not, read and pray daily. It is for your life; there is no other way: else you will be a trifler all your days."[1] Wesley's letter to John Trembath was not a legalistic requirement; it was sound spiritual guidance. It was the way to spiritual renewal. It still is.

Some of our predecessors had a phrase for it: "You have to be at the spout where the glory comes out." They meant that if we are going to actually drink of the Water of Life, we have to be at the places where it flows. Wesley's counsel to Trembath was ancient wisdom captured in a few words. Reading and praying daily comprise the two central acts of Christian devotion. While there are other means of grace and spiritual disciplines to make use of in our formation, these stand at the center regardless of which particular tradition you are part of. They are at the heart of devotional life for those of us who are United Methodist. We will explore each of them in this chapter.

However, before we do, there are two important dimensions of prayer and devotional life which must be mentioned: desire and purpose. Wesley spoke of them both in his letter to John Trembath. With respect to desire, he told Trembath to read and pray daily "whether you like it or not." The simple truth is that we cannot maintain a uniform desire day in and day out. Desire for God fluctuates. Some days we experience heights of joy; other days, we feel numb and disinterested. Understanding this is essential if we are to cultivate a genuine prayer and devotional life.

There is a difference between a "taste" for God and a "desire" for God. The fact that we are made in the image of God creates the fundamental taste for God. The psalmist described it by writing, "As a deer longs for flowing streams, so my soul longs for you, O God. My soul thirsts for God, for the living God" (42:1-2). But the desire for God can and will vary from time to time. The way to the mountain top inevitably passes through the desert. Our devotional experience will be a mixture of fulfillment and frustration. This is a mystery we cannot predict or control. Changes can come upon us suddenly and remain with us for some time.

When the changes are uplifting, I bask in the blessing. But I have also experienced periods of profound spiritual dryness and have watched others do the same. In such moments we are tempted to give up, to stop what we're doing, to think we have made some profound mistake, or perhaps even to entertain the notion that there's really nothing to this "God stuff" after all. We must reject these attitudes and refrain from ceasing our activities. Even the summons to read and pray loses its appeal sooner or later. To not know this leaves us vulnerable to being deceived or more likely, to being discouraged along the way. Wesley was giving Trembath sound spiritual guidance by telling him to keep at it whether he liked it or not.

One of the values of studying the lives of the saints is that they become real people as we get to know them better. They are not embarrassed to reveal their struggles. St. Teresa of Avila records that she experienced spiritual dryness for twenty-three years. George Fox felt the heavens to be as brass for five years. I have discovered similar experiences in such persons as Charles Spurgeon, F. B. Meyer, Evelyn Underhill, J. B. Phillips, Oswald Chambers, Thomas Merton, and Henri Nouwen. One after another, they line up to testify that desire ebbs and flows.

Most of us are familiar with John Wesley's heart-warming experience at a Moravian meeting on Aldersgate Street, the evening of May 24, 1738. Some even view the experience as his conversion to Christ. Yet eight months after this profound experience, he passed through the valley of discouragement, writing on January 4, 1739: "I affirm I am not a Christian now....that I am not a Christian at this day I as assuredly know as that Jesus is the Christ."[2] Try as he might, he could not sense any love of God or the righteousness, peace, and joy which he believed should attend a genuine experience of God. The irony of these words is increased when we note that only three days before (January 1, 1739), Wesley and six others experienced a profound outpouring of God's Spirit, complete with exceeding joy, awe, amazement, and much praise.

What is going on here? We must answer this question if we are to make sense of prayer and devotional life. What is happening is simply a clear (and somewhat extreme) example of how our sense of God and our desire for God fluctuates. By January 10th , Wesley was writing in his Journal that he was preaching and otherwise practicing his faith with meaning. This ebb and flow continued to show itself in his life and ministry, even as it will in ours.

Before we get into the details of reading and praying daily, we must be certain not to think that these exercises will enable us to maintain constant, positive desire. The spiritual life has often been referred to as "the life of God in the soul of man," but this is not an experience that never wavers over the course of our Christian journey.[3] We must take comfort in the fact that many men and women whom we admire for their faith have experienced both the "highs" of ecstasy and the "lows" of despair in their spiritual journey. We must face the fact that the same will be true of us. The desire for God wavers because the emotions needed to sustain the *feeling* of spirituality are not always present. In fact, it is often the case that the feelings leave us during the most difficult days of our lives. Therefore, it is essential to establish the foundation of prayer and devotional life on the deeper, created "taste" for God, rather than the wavering feelings of "desire" for God.

A word concerning purpose must also be given. The reason we resolutely stick to the cultivation of prayer and devotional life is found in additional words Wesley gave to Trembath: "It is for your life." I am not exaggerating when I say that God has given us the means of grace and the invitation to use them as the way of establishing and maintaining the spiritual life. Some of our predecessors called it the life of God in the human soul. Christian spiritual formation is a life-giving experience. It is an ongoing transaction of receiving God's life and consecrating our life.

To say this is to speak a great mystery, but also a great privilege. The apostle Paul described the mystery as "Christ in you, the hope of glory" (Colossians 1:27). The purpose of prayer and devotional life is nothing other than to condition ourselves in ways which enable God's Spirit to dwell within us. We say it often in the liturgy, "The risen Christ is with us." With such an amazing purpose before us, we come to view our spiritual formation as less of a duty and more of a delight. We cease seeing it as legalistic, and begin experiencing it as a relationship between God (the Lover) and us (the beloved).[4]

It is little wonder then that Wesley was so concerned to help John Trembath amend his spiritual life. By encouraging and challenging him to "read and pray daily," Wesley was attempting to put Trembath into the mainstream of Christian spirituality. For the rest of this chapter we will use

45

his twofold counsel as we seek to do the same for ourselves. There is a river of devotional life flowing deep and wide. Let's step into it!

Read

Reading is both a principle and a practice. As a principle, reading reminds us that spiritual formation is our response to and participation in that which is objective. Most of us have grown up in the past four decades—a time when subjectivity, relativism, and individual experience have become so commonplace we cannot think of life without them. Truth is now frequently defined as "what works for you." In terms of religion there is a professed tolerance which says, "I have my beliefs and you have yours; let's leave it that way." And as long as one person's (or group's) beliefs do not infringe upon another's, we are satisfied. In terms of spiritual formation, we have become a planet of "practices" often disconnected from historic traditions.[5] We have become a generation with an intense hunger for spirituality, but with almost no consensus as to what such a spirituality looks like and consists of. Fly-by-night gurus are given as much credibility as established spiritual leaders—sometimes more! We see a "pop-spirituality" where there is more interest in what's new than what's true.

John Wesley was familiar with similar spiritual dynamics in his own day. By the mid-1700's, England had been experiencing more than a century of religious, cultural, and political revolution. The seventeenth century had been torn with tragic divisions and conflicts. England was weary with controversy and sought instead a spirit of tolerance. With respect to Christian faith, there was a turning away from historic orthodoxy (Wesley called it "Scriptural Christianity") and a growing fascination with "speculative latitudinarianism."[6] One manifestation of this fascination was an "all roads lead to Rome" spirit which Wesley felt was destructive to Christian faith in general and to spiritual formation in particular.

Reading was a spiritual-guidance principle intended to restore a proper place to objectivity—to a remembrance that we are addressed by revelation, not adrift with speculation. Reading was a means of injecting back into individual and corporate life a sense of connection to and consonance with the rich tradition of Christian belief and practice. Wesley's works are filled with literally thousands of references to reading. He read privately, in groups, and sometimes as part of his public preaching and teaching. He read with others and to others. His reading spanned a wide range of subjects, and all of it was intended to establish his life in something greater than his own ideas and impressions.

I live near two very large bookstores. At almost any hour of the day or evening, each place has a large number of people browsing and reading. It is simply not true that people today have lost a taste for reading. To see the size of a Tom Clancy or Daniel Steele novel erases that notion! The questions (given a look at the shelves on which current fiction and non-fiction bestsellers are placed) are, "What kind of reading is shaping us?" and "What larger realities and traditions is our reading connecting us to?" The answer to these questions is mixed, at best. And at worst, we can often observe a disconnection between current writing and classic ideas—a fascination with the contemporary.

Good literature is being written today, and contemporary resources to advance our spiritual formation are available. Yet there is also a need to be sure that our prayer and devotional life is connected to the larger Judeo-Christian tradition, which not only precedes our time but also has significantly shaped it. The living water which we seek for our soul's nourishment flows from wells dug deeply, and long ago.

In addition to the principle which reading enforces, we must also consider the practice of reading itself. We read most often today for information or entertainment. Both of these forms of reading are legitimate and valuable. But there is a third reason for reading—for formation. Formative reading is a process which flows out of the early church into our own day. Yet it is not the type of reading taught in the schools or practiced with skill in today's culture. For most of us, it will be an activity to be learned. In our United Methodist tradition there are at least three examples which can assist us in reading formationally.

The first method is *lectio divina.* Often called "sacred reading" or "spiritual reading," it is an ancient process combining both an attitude and an activity. When we practice sacred reading, our attitude is one of desire. Dr. Susan Muto describes it this way, "As disciples of the word, we remain gently open to divine directives. We focus our attention on the text at hand and let it speak to our here and now situation."[6] Lectio divina is a way of slowing ourselves down, so that we may more attentively and thoroughly ponder what we are reading. Dr. Robert Mulholland has spoken of our attitude in life-altering language, "Lectio is a posture of approach and a means of encounter with a text that enables the text to become a place of transforming encounter with God."[7]

John Wesley expressed this same desire in one of his most passionate statements, "I want to know one thing—the way to heaven; how to land safe on that happy shore. God himself has condescended to teach the way; for this very end He came from heaven. He hath written it down in a book. O give me that book! At any price, give me the book of God! I have it: here is knowledge enough for me."[8] Wesley was, of course, referring to the Bible, but his desire to encounter

God through sacred reading extended to secondary literature as well.

Since lectio divina is something new for many of us, a brief overview is in order. I will use the Latin terminology, because these are the words you see most often in books about this kind of reading. The classic segments are lectio, meditatio, oratio, and contemplatio. In common English we would say, reading, meditating, praying, and contemplating. Before we examine each segment in particular, it is important to emphasize that they are not steps to pass through as much as they are qualities to embrace in the course of our reading. They surely overlap one another, even as they lead us through a comprehensive experience of sacred reading.

Furthermore, the segments are preceded and followed by two essential attitudes and actions: preparation and incarnation. When our predecessors practiced lectio divina, they didn't jump right into the process itself. Rather, they settled themselves through a period of silence—a kind of "Slow me down, Lord" quieting of body, mind, and spirit. They knew that in coming to any text with the desire to hear from God, they must be prepared to do so. Immediately, I am challenged. My fast-paced lifestyle often brings me to a period of reading with entirely too much "baggage" and "noise." I must learn from the saints that posture is as important as process. Silence is also a way of reminding myself that I am not reading in order to "control" the text, but rather to be addressed by it.

After the segments have been utilized, I face the need for incarnation. The written text has come alive in me; now it must be lived out through me. John Wesley surely understood this, for he wrote, "Whatever light you then receive should be used to the uttermost, and that immediately. Let there be no delay. Whatever you resolve, begin to execute the first moment you can."[9] Wesley knew that the immediate application of insight is the only thing which prevents what we have gained from either being lost or being relegated to the category of dead information.

With the proper context for lectio divina in mind, we can now move on to look at each of the segments, the first being *lectio*. This is the act of reading the text itself. In this segment we read slowly and attentively, with comparatively little regard for how much content we cover at any given time. We do not have to grasp the material or retain it in order to pass a test later on! Rather, we are seeking to enter into communion with the text—a dialog between the spirit of the text (placed in it by the author and by God who inspired the author to write it) and our spirit. A good synonym phrase is "paying attention."

John Wesley's concern for this kind of reading appears in an unsuspected place—in his desire for children to read the Bible with greatest profit. Writing to parents who would be guiding their children into the things of God, he said,

> Beware of that common, but accursed, way of making children parrots, instead of Christians. Labor that, as far as is possible, they may understand every single sentence which they read. Therefore, do not make haste. Regard not how much, but how well, to how good purpose, they read. Turn each sentence every way; propose it in every light; and question them continually on every point: If by any means they may not only read, but inwardly digest, the words of eternal life.[10]

This is one of the finest and most succinct summaries you can find regarding the segment of lectio. It applies as much to adults as to children. The following brief exercise illustrates how it works in relation to an actual text. For many of us, the opening words of Psalm 23 are deeply meaningful: "The LORD is my shepherd." Read this phrase repeatedly, each time placing an emphasis upon a different word in the text. Notice how the different emphases provide particular insight into the text itself:

The LORD is my shepherd.
The **LORD** is my shepherd.
The LORD **is** my shepherd.
The LORD is **my** shepherd.
The LORD is my **shepherd.**

What happened? How did each highlighted word bring a fresh nuance to this simple verse? Which emphasis was most important to you? Why? These are the kinds of questions which you can answer when you enter into the segment of lectio. If you were keeping a journal, you could write an extended response to the meaning you derive from each emphasis. A single word becomes a "window" through which to encounter God and to grow in grace.

Obviously, you will not read every text with this kind of word-by-word attention. But it is surely a way to slow down and see how much is contained in even a short sentence. This kind of reading illustrates the fact that we are not reading for quantity but rather for quality—not for speed but for significance. Lectio reminds us that every word holds potential for an encounter with God. And as we read larger portions, we will remain alert to those phrases which warrant our special attention.

The next segment is *meditatio*. This is the act of meditating on the text. A good synonym is "pondering." You probably moved into some brief meditation as you repeated, "The Lord is my shepherd." That's okay; the segments cannot be neatly and cleanly separated. They are parts of a dynamic whole. But strictly speaking, meditatio is distinct from lectio. Lectio is more of a style, while meditatio is more of a state of mind. And it is precisely that state of mind which we must clarify before we move on.

Meditation is a popular word today. Books, tapes, videos, and seminars abound on the subject. Meditation is widely recommended as way to reduce stress, regain focus, and make contact with the divine. Most often it has to do with an "emptying" of the mind. Physical postures and breathing techniques accompany it. Frequently, there is a mantra or meditation-word recommended to maintain centeredness. The results are renewed vigor, peace, and well-being. No doubt these qualities are beneficial, but it is essential to note that they are not what the ancients meant in using the term meditatio for the second segment of lectio divina.

Rather than an emptying of the mind, meditatio is filling the mind with the richness of the text. Rather than a passive relaxation, it is an active participation in the message. Rather than a subjective stream of consciousness, it is an objective interaction with the revelation being communicated. Rather than dealing with an imposed mantra, it is interacting with the exterior document. More than heightened consciousness and well-being, meditatio is a means to encounter God and to be formed by the influence of the relationship.

Meditation is often generated through the use of questions. Notice in the Psalms how frequently the writers use questions to stimulate reflection. When we turn to the Gospels, we see Jesus raising questions to both challenge and encourage people to get off dead-center and think more deeply about things. Return to the phrase, "The Lord is my shepherd." Use questions like these to initiate your meditation. Which word in the phrase struck you the most? Why do you think it stands out for you right now? What did the word mean when David used it? What does it mean in light of its total usage in the Bible? What meaning has it had in your life up to now? What comfort does the word provide for you? What challenges does it contain? What amendments in your life would you need to make to strengthen the influence of the word in your life right now? Questions like these set a reflective process in motion, stimulating a deeper consideration of the passage than mere reading will provide.

Meditation flows naturally into *oratio*. This is the segment of prayerful response to what we are experiencing through the text and our consideration of it. Through reading we have slowly paid attention to the passage. In meditation we have walked around it to see where our personal entry point is. Now, in prayerful response, we acknowledge that we have been addressed by God through the text, and we engage in a period of dialog with God about it. Robert Mulholland aptly describes the segment of oratio by writing, "We share with God the feelings the text has aroused in us....We pour out our heart to God in complete openness and honesty, especially as the text has probed aspects of our being and doing in the midst of various issues and relationships."[11]

I have no way of knowing what part of the phrase, "The Lord is my shepherd," spoke most to you or where you centered your meditation in relation to it. Let's suppose that it was the word "shepherd." Oratio now takes us to the prayer point of recognizing that the God of all time and space is our shepherd. We may even begin our prayerful response by saying something like, "Dear Shepherd of my life...." Then we follow with whatever expression of feelings or considerations that have touched our heart in the process of focusing on that word during our meditation. Perhaps the recollection that the Lord is our *shepherd* has evoked feelings of joy and encouragement. At other times it might give rise to feelings of pain for not having followed the one who loves us so. It doesn't matter. The process of lectio divina has led us to an encounter with some aspect of spiritual reality, and in oratio we prayerfully express our heart-response to God.

The final segment is *contemplatio*. This is at one and the same time a most important dimension and also the one that is least understood. In meditatio and oratio we have been active in relation to the text: thinking and praying. Contemplation calls us to cease our reflections and to rest in the experience we have had. This phase is more intuitive than cognitive. It is a "waiting" in an openness which says, "Lord, I have received and pondered your word to me; now, do with me what you will." Through contemplation we enter a period of literal and spiritual rest, trusting that God's word is living and active—believing it will accomplish what God wills for us. Contemplation is closely kin to that moment in Mary's life when the angel announced the amazing news that she would be the mother of Jesus, and she said, "Here am I, the servant of the Lord; let it be with me according to your word." Contemplation is simply that moment when we say from the depths of our heart, "Let it be." And from that posture of abandoned willingness, we go out to live our lives in the strength and light which lectio divina has provided.

We have given quite a bit of space in this chapter to lectio divina. Why? Because it is the bedrock for the kind of reading John Wesley was commending to John Trembath. It is the kind of reading which has shaped the lives of the saints from the time of the early church until now. It is the kind of reading which has flowed into our Wesleyan tradition, inviting the same transforming experience that shaped the early Methodists. It is a process of reading we should practice over and over until it becomes second nature to us. And when it does, we will find, in a fresh and perhaps profound way, why "searching the Scriptures" has been a major means of grace in our United Methodist tradition.

Before we move on to prayer, two additional models shed further light on this important formative process. First, John Wesley knew that there would be some who would never practice classic lectio divina because of its roots in Roman Catholicism. So, he took the same process, simplified it a bit, and commended it to the early Methodists in these words: read, mark, and inwardly digest. Reading approximated *lectio*. Marking was the synonym for *meditatio*. And inwardly digesting was the term for *contemplatio*. The act of *oratio* was assumed to be an ongoing part of the whole process. Of particular note is the fact that Wesley commended this reading process for children as well as for adults, including it in his "Prayers for Children" and instructions to parents in how best to rear their children in the ways of God.[12] He believed that children were able to practice this kind of reading and that if they did, they would grow into adulthood with a priceless ability to grow as disciples through this kind of reading.

Second, we are able to see a similar stream of spiritual reading flowing into the United Methodist tradition through the life of Jacob Albright. Like Wesley, he would have known the ancient method of lectio divina, but he would have also encountered a particular process through his Lutheran roots. Luther had said, "Divinity is nothing but a grammar of the language of the Holy Ghost."[13] In order to learn to speak this language, Luther commended a threefold process for studying theology in general and the biblical text in particular. Drawing upon the principles found in Psalm 119, Luther summarized the formative method in three terms: *oratio, meditatio,* and *tentatio.*[14]

Because we have looked at the first two, we need only to see what Luther meant by *tentatio.* In relation to classic lectio divina, tentatio is contemplation in which we "experience how right, how true, how sweet, how lovely, how mighty, how comforting is God's Word, wisdom above all wisdom."[15] But it also contains the element of trial, for Luther believed that as the word of God comes into us, the devil will likewise appear, seeking to afflict us and dissuade us from responding to the revelation. In fact, Luther believed that these trials were part of the overall formative process, enabling us to embrace the word of God precisely because we experienced it to be stronger than the deceptive words of the evil one. Coming as he did out of the Lutheran tradition, Albright would have known about lectio divina in general and more especially about the threefold pattern given him by that tradition.

By way of practical exercise, let's return one more time to the phrase, "The LORD is my shepherd." Having previously selected the term "shepherd" as our focus, let's apply possible aspects of tentatio to our reading and reflection. We might, for example, monitor our feelings as we consider that the Lord is our *shepherd*. Instead of the "rest" of contemplation, where is there some "restlessness" within us relative to it? These may come in the form of doubts, struggles based on past experience, our willful rebellion against being led by anyone other than ourselves, etc. The trial must be faced honestly, otherwise we are treating our reading in terms of avoidance or fantasy. The trial may evoke a cry for help or a confession of sin in relation to what we have encountered. Whatever the struggle, if we deal forthrightly with it, we will find the message to be true, and we will pass into the kind of "rest" we noted earlier in relation to contemplation.

Prayer and devotional life for United Methodists is rooted in this kind of formative reading. Whether we practice full-blown lectio divina or the simpler expressions commended by Wesley and Albright (from Luther), we must search the Scriptures daily in a manner that enables the written word to become the living word within us—and lived out through us. If this kind of reading is new to you, commit yourself to at least a month of trying it over and over. If it is something with which you are already familiar, look for ways to help others in your study group embrace this dimension of spiritual formation for themselves.

Pray

The fact that formative reading includes prayer is an important reminder that we cannot and must not think of Wesley's twofold counsel to Trembath as separate activities.

In a general way we can keep the two together by thinking of our reading as the period in which God speaks to us and our praying as the period in which we speak to God. The combined experience of receiving and responding forms the counsel which Wesley gave to "read and pray daily." When taken together, we can see why these two activities define the heart of our devotional life. At the same time, just as it is possible to describe specific aspects about our reading, we can also discover important truths about prayer from our tradition. The rest of the chapter focuses on the life and practice of prayer.

From a purely historical point of view, the importance of prayer in the United Methodist tradition can hardly be exaggerated. It is not too much to say that John Wesley was a man who lived to pray and prayed to live. He prayed privately and corporately, out loud and silently. He used *The Book of Common Prayer* and other prayer manuals, and yet he maintained a flexibility which included free and spontaneous prayer. He prayed at fixed times during the day, while preserving a prayerful attitude throughout the day. He studied and used the prayers of others to deepen his own prayer life, but he did not fail to express his own heartfelt petitions. His prayers contained the full range of human emotions; nothing was off-limits.[16]

But perhaps the most impressive witness John Wesley made regarding prayer was the fact that he persevered in prayer even when it was virtually meaningless to him. His private diary contains evidence that Wesley's prayers could be both "warm and effectual" and also "cold and indifferent."[17] Like you and me, he experienced times of prayer which were profound and moving. At other times, he felt as if he was merely going through the motions to no effect. But the witness which emerges in his diaries is that he kept at it for more than sixty years! His overall conclusion was that prayer is "the grand means of drawing near to God."[18]

What John Wesley personified concerning prayer was further manifested in the corporate life of early Methodism. Meetings of the Societies, Classes, and Bands were salted with prayer. The means of grace invited the people called Methodist to fixed and continuing times of personal and public praying. An examination of records from the Evangelical Reformed Church, the United Brethren in Christ, and the Evangelical Association likewise reveal a commitment to personal and corporate prayer. And Dr. Frank Baker has shown that the key elements in early-American Methodism were the preaching services, the love feasts, and the prayer meetings.[20]

This all-too-brief summary of the importance of prayer in our tradition only has meaning if we realize that the preceding data does not record history so much as it does power. The facts which we can research were simply the fuel by which the leaders and members of our predecessor churches lived and ministered. If we are to be faithful to our heritage, it is not enough to remember what they did in their day; it is necessary for us to re-engage ourselves with respect to prayer in ours. Dr. Terry Teykl is standing in the stream of our tradition when he writes, "When pastors and church leaders pray together with one heart and purpose, they are praying a price for awakening that cannot be had anywhere else."[21] If we really believe this, and if we are true to the purpose of this book, we must ask ourselves this question: "What would praying in the United Methodist tradition look like in our day?"

First, we would *recover the apostolic spirit*. The original apostles asked Jesus to teach them to pray (Luke 11:1). They had seen a depth of prayer in his life that they did not have and their religious experience had not provided. Jesus responded by giving them the Lord's Prayer (as we call it today), but it was really the apostles" prayer because it was

58

given to them to further shape and develop their praying. From then until now, this prayer has been regarded as an example of true prayer and a guide to actually shape the form and flow of personal and corporate prayer. More than a prayer to memorize and repeat, it is pattern we can use to grow in prayer. John Wesley called it the "model and standard for all our prayers."[22]

We cannot overestimate the power of the Lord's Prayer to enrich our own praying. I would encourage you to take each phrase in the prayer—perhaps one phrase per day until you work through the entire prayer—and use it to give rise to your own praying in relation to each idea. I call it "expansive praying," as we take the words of this great prayer and use it as a launching pad for our own similar expressions, petitions, and intercessions. By the way, it is possible to do the same thing with other written prayers; that's why prayer books have been (and can be) so valuable in the development of your prayer life.

As important as the Lord's prayer itself is, equally as important is the underlying attitude: "Lord, teach us to pray." In the final analysis, prayer is more an attitude than a technique. Prior to any act of prayer is the desire to pray and the commitment to pray. If you and I have that, we can find a multitude of resources to help us grow. More than providing any particular model or plan, I hope your use of this book will stimulate a deep desire to pray.

The apostolic spirit quickly became a corporate reality. Even the Lord's Prayer was given with plural words: our, us, and we. The signal was sent—there can be no genuine prayer in isolation from the rest of the body of Christ. We never pray alone. At any given moment, millions of others are praying. We always pray in the plural. Realizing this, creates the accompanying desire to pray together with others. In the Book of Acts, Luke shows us how this community spirit took hold, telling us that the first Christians devoted themselves to prayer (Acts 1:14 and 2:42).

A while back I attended a consultation lead by Lyle Schaller. Among the many things he shared with us was the fact that the fastest-growing position in the church today is that of "minister of prayer." Sometimes the person is clergy, but more often laity. The person may be full time, but usually is part-time. It is his or her task to direct the development of prayer and prayer ministry in the local church. If you are studying this book with a small group, I hope you will take time at your next meeting to consider the current reality of prayer in your church and move from there to consider how you can take concrete action to help people grow in their personal prayer life and to deepen the total congregation's life of prayer. Resources in Appendix B can help you in this effort. All of this is to say that a recovery of the apostolic spirit is part of devoting ourselves to prayer in harmony with the history and conviction of our United Methodist heritage.

Second, we would *restate the empowering sentence: "Not my will, but thine be done."* Again, this sentence has personal and congregational implications, but they both revolve around the issue of discernment. Individually and collectively we recognize that prayer is essentially about knowing and doing the will of God. We pray personally to receive guidance and power for living. We pray congregationally as a means for seeking the heart of God before we develop and execute our plans. In both cases we are involved in the practice of discernment.[23]

This is one of the reasons why prayer has often been defined more as listening than as speaking. Discernment helps root us in the conviction that God speaks the first and primary word—then, we respond both with our words and with our actions. Discernment is about the cultivation of an open, receptive heart. Rather than assembling our requests, we quite our spirits. In the first chapter we mentioned the early-morning prayer of Frank Laubach. It is an excellent example of the prayer of discernment. It can be prayed individually and modified for community prayer.

The return to discernment is occurring slowly (or so it seems) but perceptibly in churches around the world. For some it has given rise to confession and the request for God to forgive us for so often developing our plans and then subsequently asking for (or hoping) for God's blessing. For others, the revival of discernment has evoked a strengthening of community, for when we pray this way, we never know where or how the divine instruction is going to emerge. Discerning prayer levels the community and puts everyone in a spirit of submission and exploration. What results is a renewed sense that we are moving forward under a prior motivation, empowerment, and guidance. We are living out what we pray for so often in the Lord's prayer: "Thy kingdom come, thy will be done, *on earth* as it is in heaven." If we would recover vital prayer in our day, we would restate the empowering sentence.

Third, we would *restore the tangible symbol.* We pay attention to what gets our attention. Our Judeo-Christian heritage gives weight to the importance of place, location, and space. We need tangible things to evoke our participation in heavenly realities. For a growing number of churches today, the making of prayer rooms has been an important element in the renewal of prayer and prayer ministry.[24] The very act of constructing or remodeling space for prayer has an impact on the congregation. And once available, such a place becomes a center for ongoing intercession as well as a visible reminder that prayer is significant in the life of the church.

I will never forget the first time I visited John Wesley's home in London. Adjacent to his bedroom was another little room—Wesley's prayer room. No larger than a small closet, this room served as a tangible invitation for Wesley to rise and pray in the morning, to pray during the day, and to be a place to go before retiring for the night. As I entered in that little space, I went to my knees as naturally as I was breathing. The place itself was saturated with the prayers which Wesley offered there and which countless others have lifted to God while visiting the home. We need similar sacred spaces in our homes and churches as we recover vital prayer in contemporary United Methodism.

Fourth, we would *relate to the global experience*. A phenomenal, worldwide prayer movement is sweeping across the earth in our generation. We must not be left out of it. We must connect with it. Not every feature of the current prayer revival will appeal or relate to every person or congregation in United Methodism. But there are plenty of avenues leading into this obvious work of God in our day. We must become familiar with the contemporary prayer revival and connect with it in ways that are authentic and meaningful for us personally and for our local churches.

In the United States alone it is estimated that 150,000 congregations are currently participating in this prayer movement in some way, with others being added along the way. But the movement itself is by no means contained in one particular country of the world. In fact, some of the most powerful expressions are happening outside the United States. The United Methodist Church is a "connectional church," and that means far more than paying our apportionments, or even joining with other United Methodists. It means connecting with the larger body of Christ to receive the blessings of that association as well as to reflect the dynamics which spiritual ecumenism provides. The current, global prayer revival is a marvelous opportunity to do just that.[25]

Finally, we would *reinforce our leaders through protective intercession*. Too many of our clergy and lay leaders are lonely ministers practicing lonely ministry. They are more likely to hear words of criticism than words of support. They are preyed on more than they are prayed for! If United Methodism is to recover its spiritual vitality and power, this must stop. And the only way it can stop is for people to say, "Enough!" and begin to undergird leaders with specific and sustained prayer support.

This means forming intercessory prayer groups for leaders not directly in the congregation: bishops, superintendents, heads of general agencies, conference lay and clergy leaders, and support staff at every level of the church's life. It also means forming prayer support teams to actually pray for and with local leaders. As few as seven persons, each willing to pray one day a week is all it takes; in fact, you can begin with even fewer than that! The point is to cover our leaders with ongoing intercession as they carry out the duties of their ministries.

We have allowed the enemy to erode the strength and spirit of our leaders for too long. We must surround them with protective and encouraging prayer. I have lost count of the number of pastors in particular who have told me that they have no tangible prayer support. Of course, they believe they are being prayed for by some in the church, but they themselves do not know who their supporters are. We provide a great blessing when we move this kind of praying from the realm of being vague and nonspecific to that of being an ongoing part of the church's life.

These are only a few ways in which we can participate in the current, worldwide prayer renewal. Hopefully, they will be enough to enable you to make a start. Contemporary involvement in prayer will enable you to experience for yourself why John Wesley called prayer the chief means of grace. Practicing the life of prayer will confirm why prayer stands at the heart of any understanding of the devotional life in our United Methodist heritage. Most of all, engaging in prayer will bring you into the presence of the One who loves you more than you can imagine—the One who wants to relate to you, and then through you to others.

When John Wesley counseled John Trembath to "read and pray daily," he was offering him the two best ingredients he knew for centering life in the things of God. But unfortunately, this was not one of early Methodism's success stories. What little we know of Trembath indicates that he did not follow Wesley's advice. Although he started out as one of the more popular itinerant preachers in Methodism, he eventually faded out of the picture. Despite several attempts on Wesley's part to exhort him to give heed to self-discipline, he seems to have largely ignored the advice.

This may seem like a strange and rather negative way to end this chapter, but it serves to remind us all that the tried-and-true elements we have examined in this chapter cannot be long avoided without consequences. Erosion of soul follows the abdication of a commitment to discipline. John Trembath is only one illustration of that historic fact. If we are to be in the stream of prayer and devotional life in the United Methodist tradition, we will find our place among those who have determined to "read and pray daily." Like them, we will realize it is for the sake of our life.

Living It Out

1. Which part of this chapter spoke most to you? Why was it an important message for you to hear right now? What is one concrete action you can take to make that part more meaningful in your prayer and devotional life?

2. Train yourself in the art of lectio divina. Use whatever passages you like. Spend five-day periods studying your choices, using one element of lectio divina each day. On the fifth day, write out a summary of how this passage has become more real to you as well as how you now

intend to live it out in your daily life. It will not be long before these elements will feel more natural to you, and once they do, you will be amazed at how you will begin to read "beneath the surface" to absorb deeper and more personal elements of what you are reading.

3. Was it a new thought for you to realize you are living in a generation when a renewal of prayer is occurring all over the world? How does this idea impact you? Consider taking one of the suggested means of participating in the worldwide prayer revival and practicing it for thirty days. A month is a good length of time to incorporate a new spiritual discipline into your life. Keep a journal close at hand to record your experiences as you commit to prayer in this way.

4. Look at your calendar. About a month from now, plan at least a two-hour period for retreat and reflection. If you are making a commitment to renew your reading and praying, that will be a good time to take stock of what is happening in your life as a result. Remember that in spiritual formation one thing leads to another. Your reflection period is not meant to "finalize" or "analyze" anything, but rather to pay attention to where you are in the overall growth process. You will see some gains as well as some places where you have not made much progress. This is normal. The point is to keep paying attention to your development and continuing to follow your heart as you move from one degree of devotion to another.

Chapter 3

Get Connected!

IF YOU HAVE been a member of the United Methodist Church for any length of time, you've probably heard the statement, "We are a connectional church." It often comes up in a discussion of our stewardship, especially as it relates to the paying of apportionments to support the work of our denomination beyond the local church. But it is a richer and deeper idea than simply giving money. As United Methodists, we see ourselves as a body of believers "connected" with each other in a fellowship of love, accountability, and mutual ministry.

The idea of and commitment to connectionalism is as old as the Methodist movement itself. When John Wesley chose the name "United Societies" for the movement, even the title spoke to the nature of early-Methodist associations. In preparing to write this chapter, I conducted some research on Wesley's use of the term "connection." I discovered that his writings are filled with it. In fact, it could be argued that it is one of Wesley's favorite words. He saw "connections" between ideas, between doctrines, between churches, and between people. He wanted the early Methodists to be "in connection" with him, with each other, and with the larger body of Christ.

The precedents for this view of the Christian life lay in his own background. He referred to the beginnings of Methodism as happening in his mother's kitchen in Epworth and in the Holy Club at Oxford. He carried precious memories of Susanna's weekly private times with each of her children and of her assembling parishioners on Sunday evenings for instruction and guidance. He had lived through the evolution of the Holy Club at the university (including its ridicule), coming to see it as a virtual laboratory of practical divinity. Both of these experiences were expressions of connectionism. As it became clear that God was calling him to begin the Methodist movement, they shaped his thinking regarding its nature and mission. From both his mother and his fellow students Wesley saw the power of sustained relationships—relationships centered in Christ and in a common commitment to live for him.

As Methodism advanced, he likewise observed the deformative dangers that emerged when connectionism was either absent or abandoned. When individuals or groups did not live in connection, he saw it as the usual and primary cause of their decline.[1] It was the spiritual disease that made people "sick" in their relationship with God and with one another. When certain individuals no longer wanted to be active members of the group, Wesley "quarantined" them— put them out of the Methodist connection until they were ready, willing, and able, to be part of formative fellowship. He did not take such action as a means to make Methodism legalistic or exclusive, but rather to reinforce his unwavering belief in and commitment to the power of Christian associations. As a physician of the soul, he also knew the infective influence of negativism or shallow piety—the deformative dynamic that even one half-hearted person can have on the rest. So, he established early Methodism on the principles and practices of "connectionalism." To be connected lies at the heart of the corporate life of our United Methodist tradition.

With respect to prayer and devotional life, connectionalism is clearly seen in the means of grace. In the instituted means of grace called Christian conference, we have the basis for the formational and the structural aspects of early-Methodist devotion. We will use these two elements to form the major sections of this chapter. We will explore the classical formation which occurred in the groups, and we will see how the groups were organized to facilitate the work of God. But it is also important to see that the prudential means of grace create a connection. They bind us together in an ethical fashion—a connection in which we do no harm to one another, do all the good we can to each other, and practice the disciplines of the spiritual life in community. Simply put, it is impossible for us to understand ourselves as United Methodists apart from a clear sense of connectionalism. We cannot rightly understand or practice prayer and devotional life in consonance with our heritage apart from it. Hence, the title of this chapter, "Get Connected!" It would surely be Wesley's exhortation to us.

It is an exhortation which can hardly be overemphasized in contemporary culture whose roots are planted in pervasive individualism. Even in the eighteenth century, John Wesley noted that when people lost their formative connections, they became "cold and dead."[2] Things haven't changed. Something counterproductive happens when we lose our sense of connection with one another. Dr. David Wells has observed this trend in our society and writes, "the internal ethic of the self—what is right for **me**—has become the means by which all external standards, external controls, and external expectations are remitted."[3] He goes on to show in his excellent book, how the exaltation of the "self" has had a massive and debilitating effect on society—and on the church to the extent that it has participated in and reflected this preoccupation. The loss of connectionalism (then and now) strikes at the heart of our tradition. Both Wesley and contemporary observers rightly point out that the loss of connection leads to the erosion and eventual abandonment of holiness. Without connectionalism, we lose sight of both a theology and a life which has a moral basis and a commitment to virtue. The sinews of religious and social life are created and intertwined by connection.

This conviction leads us to Christian conference in the instituted means of grace. Wesley believed that God mediates grace when we come together for religious conversation and interaction. In holding this belief, he was merely echoing the biblical notions of community: the church as the people of God and the exhortation not to neglect meeting together (Hebrews 10:25)—to name only two illustrations of the principle. In this kind of fellowship, private revelations were challenged and tested, common life was shaped and directed, and mission was envisioned and acted out. Getting connected was the immediate need and the necessary result for any and all who tasted the goodness of the Lord.

Wesley was so convinced of this that he wove it into his earliest contacts with people. Wherever he preached, he called for response. It was not the response of conversion, though he was surely not against that! Rather, it was an invitation to respond to God's grace more in terms of awakening. Wesley's invitation at the end of his sermons was in effect asking, "Who among you is tired of living in sin and living for self? Who is here who is ready to flee the wrath to come and live for God?" Those who so responded were immediately welcomed in the Methodist fellowship. A meeting of the Society was called that very evening, and the newly-identified seekers were made to feel welcome and set on the journey of Christian formation. In fact, it can be said that the first discipling action in early Methodism was connection, not conversion. The connection was grounded in foundational principles of classical spiritual formation. We want to take the first major section of this chapter to highlight what some of them were.

Classical Formation

Wesley's commitment to connectionalism was similar to an iceberg. Much of it was "below the surface"—rooted in historic spiritual-development principles which he did not always discuss at length, but which were clearly at work. Connectionalism was also one of the primary ways Wesley avoided sectarianism and any notions of pride that might cause Methodism to stand apart from the larger expressions of Christianity. From the beginning he sought the formation of Christians, not Methodists.[4] The question for us is, "How did he practice classical formation in the Methodist Connection?" This is a book about life-enriching *practices*. To see some of the things Wesley did in his first groups can shed light as we attempt similar things today.

First, Wesley formed people along lines similar to historic spiritual orders. I happen to be among those Wesley scholars who believe John Wesley was quietly but consciously organizing early Methodism as founders of spiritual orders in Roman Catholicism had done.[5] For example, *The General Rules of the United Societies* (1743) which served as the organizational document for the Methodist movement had precedents in earlier orders such as the Benedictines. And there are significant parallels between early Methodism and the Franciscans.[6]

This first point may seem a bit abstract and cumbersome for a book like this, but I have felt compelled to include it. It has relevance for us today. One of Wesley's favorite maxims (common, he said, in early Christianity) was this, "the soul and the body make a man, and the spirit and discipline make a Christian."[7] This phrase is very similar to the twofold concern of historic spiritual orders to cultivate fervency of spirit and tenacity of discipline in their members. It is also a statement which reflects the importance of both soul and body in the development of healthy and authentic people. The founders of historic spiritual orders were likewise devoted to prayer (for the soul) and labor (for the body) in their communities. By beginning with General Rules, Wesley was tipping his hand, revealing a largely hidden but clearly obvious commitment to the creation of the Methodist movement as a disciplined order.

But even when we see what he was doing, it is still easy to ask, "What in the world does this have to do with prayer and devotional life in contemporary United Methodism?" I imagine there are a number of ways to answer the question. For now, let me provide only two. For one thing, the notion of a spiritual order tells us we are not creating a social club. Being connected is not holding one more membership in something nice and enjoyable, though we hope small-group formation will be both. Viewing our connection as a disciplined order takes us beyond socialization to spiritual formation. It takes us to the two great commandments: loving God and loving one another. These are the primary reasons we get together, regardless of the other things we benefit from and enjoy.

I cut my teeth in the seventies on a concept of small-group ministry which made "refreshments" an essential part of the weekly meeting. But today, small-group ministry has matured to the point of seeing cookies and finger food as secondary. Many groups don't serve refreshments at all. Those that do have them much more on the periphery of the group experience than in earlier times. Now don't misunderstand me; there's nothing wrong with providing some food and drink when your group meets. In fact, depending on when you meet, it may be a very natural thing to do.

Socializing with chips and dip can also provide an environment of safe sharing and getting to know the other people in your group. It's a matter of focus and not allowing something to sidetrack you from the deeper reasons you have chosen to assemble. Viewing what you do in relation to a spiritual order helps you remember that more important than having food present is having Christ present.

Additionally, viewing our formation as a spiritual order also means we understand our development to be occurring *within* the larger denomination—not apart from it. The founders of spiritual orders never saw their groups as substitute Churches, but rather as "little churches" (ecclesiola) inside the "big church" (ecclesia). The big church provided the context, content, and continuity for growth in the little churches. In turn, the groups served as seedbeds for the creation of a devotional dynamic which helped renew the life of the larger church.

Applied to your situation today, this means that you will be attentive to the attitudes which are emerging in your group. If an attitude of spiritual pride sprouts, you will nip it in the bud. If people come to the group but stop going to regular church activities, you will challenge them to renew their vows to uphold the church with their prayers, presence, gifts, and service. If they see their participation in the group as an end rather than a means, you will keep clarifying the larger perspective of the "little church" within the "big church." Before Wesley died in 1791, he had already seen Methodist groups develop these kinds of deformative dynamics. Whenever he saw them, he sternly criticized them. Sometimes he would even replace the leaders of the groups when he saw them creating associations that were too self-serving. I'm convinced it's one of the reasons he rejected for a long time any attempts to transform the United Societies into an actual church. It's another indication that he was creating a spiritual order.

Related to this, the founders of spiritual orders did not wait for the whole church to be involved or naively assume the entire church would be supportive. Classical spiritual formation does not presume that the whole church will be equally concerned about or devoted to the kind of things we're describing in this book and in the series in which it is a part. Nor does classical spiritual formation wait until there is some kind of legislative mandate for the whole denomination to be universally concerned about prayer and devotional life. Instead, the invitation goes forth and finds response in certain places and people more than in others. Those who recognize the significance of a deeper commitment to Christian spirituality join together in a "spirited" and "disciplined" journey to grow in the grace of God. And in so doing, whether formal or not—organizational or not, they become a spiritual order within the larger church.

Worked out practically, this means that your congregation must extend the invitation to a journey of deepening discipleship without expecting (much less demanding) there to be wholesale acceptance and participation. You cannot mandate spiritual formation. To require it is to turn the "spirit" into manipulation and the "discipline" into legalism. This only fosters deformative pride among those who join (easily viewing themselves as the "really spiritual ones" in the church) and promotes unnecessary and unhealthy reactions from those who do not participate. What started out with a good intention ends up producing a divided house and a contentious spirit within the congregation. By contrast, historic spiritual orders clearly show that their authenticity, vitality, and influence are born out of quiet, voluntary participation—not boisterous, self-referent activities.

Here are two large reasons why we must include the idea of a spiritual order in a book on the prayer and devotional life of United Methodists today. This is why many small groups in the church today have started well and ended poorly. Keeping your connection in relation to an understanding of historic orders will do something for you both as a member of your group and as a leader of groups, should God call you to that ministry. And that's why this point must be included in a book seeking to promote the renewal of prayer and devotional life in United Methodism. Viewing our connectionalism in this way creates and enables us to live within a healthy vision of the whole church.

Second, Wesley incorporated a version of spiritual guidance into the Methodist movement. His training for the Anglican priesthood educated him in the historic concept of spiritual guidance. His service as a curate at Wroot, his ministry with students as a Fellow at Lincoln College (Oxford University), and his term of missionary ministry in Georgia all contained elements of spiritual guidance. And by his own accounts, he had also seen this ministry exercised in both his parents.

So, when he formally began the Methodist movement in 1739, it is not surprising that he commenced with spiritual conversations to a small group of people on Thursday evenings in London.[8] As the movement grew, it soon became evident that he could not properly care for the needs of the people who were attaching themselves to Methodism. He turned to what he knew best to sustain them—spiritual guidance, and that most often by laity. The leaders of the societies, classes, and bands were not formally trained in spiritual guidance, but they functioned as such nonetheless. The grand principle which gave rise to their ministry was "watching over one another in love"—a clear reference to the spirit and methodology of sound guidance.

Translated into contemporary United Methodism, the recovery of this element of classical formation calls for a new generation of persons engaged in accountable discipleship.[9] As in Wesley's day, this kind of spiritual guidance is not so much about techniques as it is about commitments to look after one another in ways that enable an authentic and vital continuation of the Christian journey. Because this book aims at practical expressions of our heritage, let's turn to some expressions of what "watching over one another in love" means for spiritual guidance today.

Most of all, it means that the leaders adopt a posture of servanthood, not superiority. No greater danger attends the recovery of spiritual guidance than for the leaders to assume an attitude of attainment and operate a program of guidance which says in effect, "Let's see how quickly you can become as spiritual as I am!" We made some reference to this in the first chapter, but here we are again staring it in the face. Watching over one another in love means that the goal of guidance is not for others to become like us, but for all of us to become like Christ.

It also means that we pay attention to the weakest links. A posture of superiority hands out awards to those who do well in the system. Watching over one another in love means we gather around the strugglers and become their cheerleaders. In fact, if we are doing this really well, these folks are never made to feel "weak" at all—only pilgrims on a way of formation that none of us is able to achieve ultimately or perform perfectly. In the next section of this chapter we will see how Wesley paid particular attention to this need.

Watching over one another in love means that the fruit of the Spirit (Galatians 5:22-23) takes precedence over the gifts of the Spirit. The hallmark of Christian formation is growth in the grace of God which produces love, joy, peace, patience, kindness, goodness, gentleness, faithfulness, and self-control. These are the qualities we use to answer the question, "How am I doing?" The great paradox of the spiritual life is that the "doing" issue is settled through the "being" dimension. It is impossible for any of the nine aspects of the fruit to exist apart from an actual lived-out expression of them. Classical formation has always grounded itself in the cultivation of virtue.[10]

Wesley's third expression of classical formation was comprehensive care. Stanley Ayling describes it in these words, "the business was of course the saving of souls; but there was the important sideline of saving bodies too."[11] I would agree with Ayling's assessment of priority, but I do not believe early Methodism's concern for the total welfare of people was by any means a "sideline." Rather, it was a living out of Wesley's conviction that there can be no personal holiness without social holiness. Early in his life he had been greatly affected while reading the biography of the French mystic, Count Jean-Baptiste de Renty. De Renty was a devout Christian who gave large amounts of time to prayer and equal amounts of time to works of mercy with people in need. Wesley saw in the life of this man the example he longed to hold for himself and, later, the model he wanted the Methodist movement to emulate.

Consequently, alongside evangelism (not a sideline to it), we see Wesley opening dispensaries for the ill, providing schools for the uneducated, and instructing people in healthy eating, sound sleep patterns, and regular exercise programs. He offered interest-free loans to the needy, medicine to the sick, and vocational training to the unemployed. He had a special concern for the poor, the sick, those in captivity, and abused children. He used the power of his pen to write pamphlets calling the affluent to accountability and the wayward to righteousness. Many of his sermons were about the practical outworkings of Christian faith, particularly to those in need. In doing these things, he felt he was connecting the Methodist movement to the deepest and best of early Christianity.[12]

He financed this care through the sale of his writings and the special generosity of a few Christian philanthropists. But the genius of his efforts lay in the stewardship system established within the societies. Members were expected to give a penny a week to the care of others. Society leaders collected these offerings as they visited from house to house. Some of the funds remained in the local society to meet the needs of its own members and those within its reach. The remainder was sent to the conference, combined with the rest of the contributions from the United Societies, and then put to work for the common good. His personal principle to gain all he could, save all he could, and give all he could soon became the motivating force for the ministry of comprehensive care by all the Methodist people. It was an integral part of Wesley's classical formation.

A fourth expression must also be mentioned—Wesley's insistence that the early Methodists be nurtured in their faith through the reading of classical literature. He urged his preachers to read at least five hours a day, and the annual conference minutes sometimes contained the reading lists preachers were to follow. Laity, likewise, were encouraged to read time-tested works. His letters frequently contained references to the books he was reading, and he never hesitated to recommend a particular book as a means of meeting spiritual need. Taking this principle as-a-whole, it is clear Wesley believed that God had already spoken powerfully guiding words through the writings of the saints. He did not have to say things over again; he had only to put his people in touch with what had already been published.

Nevertheless, he realized that some of "the choicest pieces of practical divinity" (Wesley's term for the kind of literature he felt best shaped the souls of people) were not easy to come by, especially to those of limited finances. So, he set about on his most comprehensive publishing venture, A Christian Library.[13] The project was a monumental editorial effort, but it was all aimed to provide people with a collection of classic spiritual formation literature "going down to the depth, and describing the height, of Christianity"—a series which would "write [God's] love in every reader's heart."[14]

Writing God's love in every heart surely summarizes what Wesley intended for the spiritual formation of the people called Methodist. But he knew that this kind of "writing" does not take place apart from something to write with and something to write on; that is, classical formation requires tangible structures. The spirit of Methodist devotion needed a system to facilitate it. Christian conference was a means of grace to communicate the message and concretize the movement, variously known as the United Societies and the Methodist Connection. The second half of this chapter focuses on the Methodist organization.

Concrete Structures

Years ago, I was leading a seminar on early-Methodism, attempting to show what we can learn from it for the good of the church today. One of the participants asked me, "What do you consider the genius of Wesley?" I had never considered the question before, and I don't recall that I had a real good answer at the time. But the question burned itself into me, until today I have no idea how much time I've spent pondering it. The answer I now give is this, "the genius of Wesley and the early Methodists was in the blending of spirit and structure." Although so far as I know, John Wesley never wrote down his strategy, it is clear that he had one. He was unable to "do theology" in a vacuum; he had to have a vehicle. Convictions had to become concrete. Methodism's substance demanded a system.

Examples abound. Wesley believed that children were being mistreated in English society, preyed upon in part due to a lack of learning. So, he founded the Kingswood School for the education of children. He believed women were too much ignored in traditional English schools, so at the Foundery in London he had classes for them just as he had for men. He lamented the sad state of medical care in many parts of the country, so he studied medicine himself and published *Primitive Physic* to promote healing for persons who had insufficient access to doctors. He believed that coal miners were overlooked by the church, so he rose early to preach to them as they entered the mines and otherwise cared for their souls. He believed that many people were starving because food staples were being diverted to other uses, so he wrote a tract to farmers to use their grain to save people, not just to feed their animals and make beer. He believed that people were lost without Christ, so he recruited a cadre of Methodist preachers and told them, "You have nothing to do but save souls." It goes on and on.

And nowhere is this blend of spirit and structure more evident than in the organization of Methodism into societies, classes, and bands. As we shall see, each group had a connection to the theology of grace and was designed to be a means for facilitating the flow of grace into human life. The point of this section is not to launch a "back to the eighteenth century" movement in United Methodism today, but rather to foster a sober examination of our structures to see if we are still (as one interpreter of American Methodism put it) "organizing to beat the devil."[15] We cannot go back to some caricatured golden-age of Methodism, but we can use our heritage as a window through which to look to see if we are fostering the kind of connectionalism and Christian conference that will result in the enhancement of prayer and devotional life for contemporary United Methodists.

As I have pointed out previously, any examination of the concrete formative structures of Methodism must begin with the Church—capital "C" intended. I do not want to go back over ground we've already covered, but I do want to reinforce this point as we examine the concrete structures of the Methodist movement. Wesley did not start a church, but he did organize Methodism to draw life from it and contribute life to it. The official structures of Methodism make no sense without a solid theology of the church and real-life congregations underneath them. Anyone who tries to tell you that John Wesley was some kind of "renegade" when it comes to the church is lying to you! From beginning to end, he was a devoted priest of the Church of England. On May 6, 1788, slightly over three years before his death, he wrote some of his clearest words about this to his friend, Henry Moore, "I am a Church-of-England man; and as I said fifty years ago so say I still, in the Church I will live and die, unless I am thrust out."[16]

These were not the emotion-charged sentiments of an old man, they were the bedrock convictions he had held for more than five decades. The whole scheme of Methodism was predicated and sustained on the unwavering belief that God had brought it into existence to contribute to the church, not separate from it. In the same letter to Henry Moore, Wesley was still trying to forbid Methodists to conduct their meetings at hours which conflicted with the services of the church. What we are about to say regarding the concrete structures of early Methodism must be said on the sure foundation of belief in the Church. The life-enriching practices you derive from reading this book must be exercised in the context of your membership in the church. Having reiterated this foundational truth, we can safely and profitably move on to look at the groups which made up the Methodist system of spiritual formation.

We begin with the societies, Wesley's first expression of Methodism. The Society Movement in England had created both civic and religious groups some forty years prior to the beginnings of the United Societies.[17] There were societies in the civic realm organized for such things as the reformation of manners, the alleviation of poverty, the propagation of the gospel in foreign lands, and the promotion of Christian knowledge. There were societies within the Church of England, likewise organized for a variety of purposes. In one way or another—whether distinctively religious or not—they came into being to foster holiness of heart and life.[18] When Wesley began to nurture people who sought his guidance, his use of this model (including his decision to call the groups societies) was a consciously considered way to connect with something essentially positive in English society and deemed by some to be a genuine movement of God.

His purposes in beginning with this structure were related to prevenient grace, the first wave of grace washing on the beach of the human soul. If spiritual formation begins in one's awakening to the reality of sin and the need for righteousness, there must be a group that receives people who "desire to flee the wrath to come" but don't know much more than that. The societies of early Methodism existed to represent and mediate that kind of grace. They were groups made up of both men and women. They gathered to sing, to pray, and to be taught the Bible in a systematic fashion.[19] In cities there were many such groups, sometimes rather large. In rural areas there might only be a small society in an entire region. But regardless of number or size, the societies were the foundational structure of Methodism. "Upon reflection," Wesley wrote, "I could not but observe, this was the very thing which was from the beginning of Christianity."[20]

Looking at our system today, we must ask, "Where is the place for those who know little other than that they have been awakened to their need of God?" They may have little interest in or experience of the church itself, but they have a hunger for the Almighty. They may have all sorts of misconceptions about the church, but they have a nagging need for "something more" in their lives. They may view mainline, denominational Christianity as irrelevant, but they sense a stirring in their souls. They may not feel "safe" or even "welcome" in the church, but they long to know God's forgiveness and acceptance. Where do they go? How are they cared for in our United Methodist structures? What ports of entry exist in your congregation for people at this stage of the journey? These are crucial questions to deal with if we are to manifest prayer and devotional life in the Wesleyan tradition.

Church is not the first step for people today anymore than it was for many in the eighteenth century. Wesley knew that and provided another structure where people could find acceptance, support, and the kind of instruction that would connect their longings to God's love. The societies met in places other than the church and, at times, other than regular worship. They took things slowly and received people "just as they were." People soon realized that in attending the society meetings they had nothing to fear and much to gain. "Fleeing the wrath to come" was not merely an exercise in getting the bad stuff out but also a process of getting the good stuff in. And it happened—just as a theology of grace taught it would and Wesley believed it would.

Yet, as important as the societies were in the scheme of Methodist organization, they did not turn out to be the central structure of the movement. That place came to be occupied by the class meeting. Howard Snyder is correct: "The class meeting was the cornerstone of the whole edifice."[21] For one thing, it was the structural midwife in which most of the new births occurred. In the societies people were encouraged to flee the wrath to come and to seek after a transforming experience with God through Christ. But it was normally at least three months of meeting in a class that brought the earnest seeker to the point of conversion. Why? Because the class meetings were smaller, usually no more than a dozen men and women meeting together. It was a place where personal questions could be dealt with, fears removed, anxieties relieved, testimonies shared—all of which God used to deliver saving grace to repentant persons. Class meetings were essentially house churches meeting in the neighborhoods of the members. Convenience coupled with conviction to produce conversion. Within four years of the beginning of Methodism (that is, by 1746) the class meeting was the clearly established structure for Methodist formation.

It was also the nurturing structure which most clearly made it from Great Britain to the United States. In 1798, Thomas Coke and Francis Asbury summarized the significance of the classes by writing, "In short, we can truly say, that through the grace of God our classes form the pillars of our work, and as we have before observed, are in a considerable degree our universities for the ministry."[22] By 1850 this picture was changing, and the class meeting went into a decline from which it has never fully recovered.

The class meeting is likewise the structure which found expression in the sister denominations which preceded the organization of United Methodism. The *Constitution and Ordinances of the Evangelical Reformed Church* (1785) gave detailed instructions for conducting class meetings. Preachers in the United Brethren in Christ Jesus (c. 1800) met in gatherings virtually synonymous with class meetings. Predecessors such as Jacob Albright and Philip Otterbein led class meetings in their homes. In 1851, John Miley, the preeminent Methodist theologian at the time captured the significance of the class meeting, not only for the Methodist Church but for all its spiritual relatives, "Class meetings should . . . be dear to all the friends of Methodism, and should receive the hearty approval and support of all in her communion."[23]

Again we must ask, "Where is the place in our system where people can be dealt with at a level which enables them to move from doubt to faith? Where is the place for people to be nurtured until they can say, 'I believe in Jesus Christ as Lord' "? Please note that it was not at the altar of the church where most people became Christians; it was the confident and confidential fellowship of the class meeting. The altar surely has its place in the total scheme of things, but it is more a carryover from the camp meeting and the revival than the Methodist system of formation. The class meeting provided a weekly occasion to see how people were progressing—a place where they could receive advice, challenge, comfort, encouragement, and the prayers of their fellow members. And as in the societies, with respect to prevenient grace, God used the class meetings as a means to offer converting grace to people.

At this point in our examination of formative structures, we have more to draw on than any other feature. We have lived through the evolution of the small-group movement, with many features akin to the role class meetings played in early Methodism. Available resources abound to help us establish and sustain this dimension of connectionalism. And evidence is mounting to support the belief that small-groups are the basis for more pervasive corporate vitality in the church.

But Wesley did not stop there. He incorporated the band meetings into the structure of early Methodism. He had seen these in operation as far back as 1735 when he first encountered the Moravians in Georgia. Applied to the Methodist movement, they were the structure designed to enable sanctifying grace to manifest itself in those who had professed faith in Christ and were now "going on to perfection." There needed to be a group where devout disciples could focus on issues pertaining to holiness of heart and life. The bands provided that place, but not in the same way as the societies and classes had done. Bands were divided by gender, marital status, and, sometimes, by vocation. The principle being expressed was this: nurture in godliness occurs best when people of like condition meet together to speak personally about holy living and hold each other accountable to it. In keeping with the intimacy of the band meetings, the groups rarely numbered more than five or six.

The bands concentrated on the encouragement of members to abstain from evil, to be particularly zealous for good works, to meet weekly to share the true state of their souls, and to ask for counsel and fervent prayer where amendments were needed. The groups covenanted for confidentiality, enabling them to deal personally, specifically, and deeply with known sins, besetting temptations, uncertainties in matters of belief and practice, and any other issues pertinent to a person's spiritual progress. The tone was one of confession and amendment, but not in an atmosphere of judgment or critique. Instead, band members came together claiming a participation in the sanctifying grace of God which enables honest assessment on the one hand and promotes hopeful growth in grace on the other.

Not surprisingly, there were fewer bands in early Methodism than classes. Not everyone was ready and able to participate in this kind of regular soul-searching. But for those who were, Wesley believed that the bands would do much to promote holy living among the people called Methodist. Furthermore, bands were not established in some places because the class meetings served both purposes. In fact, some classes would begin with men and women meeting separately, using a band format, and coming together for a group process more akin to what we described in the class meeting. In time, the bands largely disappeared, being dropped in some places or subsumed into the classes in others.

Today, the mentoring movement is an expression of the commitment found in early-Methodist bands. Most mentoring groups are small. They are made up of people who share similar ages and stages of life. Men meet with men, and women with women. The goal of contemporary mentoring groups is not the dissemination of basic information or the sharing of fundamental experience, but rather a probing into person-specific issues—often those which threaten to inhibit godly living. As we compare United Methodism today with our historic roots, we must look for places of intimacy and confidentiality where a few people can "band together" to personalize their spiritual formation agenda. At some point in the cultivation of prayer and devotional life, there must be a place where the focus shifts from subject matter to human beings. Where do you find such places in your congregation? What difference is this kind of group making in the lives of those who participate in it?

At this point, you might be ready to say, "Enough!" But in order to lay out the complete picture, two other structures must be briefly mentioned. The first was the select society. Wesley knew there would be those few people who, at any given time, were poised for particular growth in grace. The select societies were available for those who were especially ready to "zero in" on particular aspects of discipleship development. Likewise, he knew there would be those who (for a variety of reasons) were struggling—maybe even losing ground. The penitent bands were there for them; places of quiet counsel away from the spotlight of judgment or criticism—another "safe place" in the Methodist formation system. These little groups were frequently the means God used to bring people back into vital fellowship with Christ and each other.

These last two groups raise important questions, "Where in our church do we have places for people who are ready to make special progress?" and "Where do we have places for people to be encouraged when they fail?" With respect to the first question, we must be responsive to the expressed needs of growing Christians and provide focused growth opportunities for them. In terms of the second question, we must admit that sometimes the only category we have for strugglers is that of "inactive member"—a phrase hardly worthy of sons and daughters of Wesley! Most congregations will find this second question more difficult to answer.

We have not developed a theology of grace with respect to restoration to the extent we have with other aspects of our doctrine. And we need a fresh development of "confessional places" within the existing structures of our congregations. This could easily be a topic for your study group to consider what you are doing (or might do) to reflect this dynamic which so greatly affects prayer and the devotional life.

I hope this chapter has given you a clearer and deeper sense of "connectionalism" in relation to spiritual formation in our United Methodist tradition. I hope you will never again think of the word as having only to do with money—even though Christian stewardship is surely part of a genuine devotional life, as we have seen. Rather, I hope you will see getting connected as an indispensable element in the cultivation of authentic Christian spirituality. As you bring your personal reading of this chapter to a close, you may want to use these moments to reflect upon your own degree of connectedness within the church. If it is where it should be, consider if there are ways you can use your experience as a testimony for others. If it is not what it should be, perhaps this is a good time to responded to the invitation of Christ to . . . get connected!

Chapter 4

Go On!

As SOON AS I was old enough, I joined the Cub Scouts. By the time I was a junior in high school I had moved through the Boy Scouts into Explorer Scouting. I was only two merit badges away from becoming an Eagle Scout—swimming and life-saving. I had resigned myself to the fact that I would never earn them because I had not learned to swim. By my junior year in high school this was an embarrassment to me, and I had made peace with the fact that I would forever be an "almost Eagle."

But my scoutmaster, Edd Smart, had not accepted that fact. He had other ideas. When summer camp drew near, he phoned to ask me if I planned to go. I made up some kind of story, excusing myself even though Camp Tonkawa had been a part of my summers for a number of years. Edd already knew what I was unwilling to tell him: I was staying away from camp because I didn't want to be the only junior in high school relegated to the "beginner" end of the swimming pool. So, he said to me, "If I could arrange it so that you don't have to swim, would you like to go to camp?" I told him that would be good and that I really would enjoy going to camp with my friends. He said he would work things out, and when the day came, I was on the scout bus heading for Camp Tonkawa.

No sooner had I set foot on the campground before Edd motioned to one of the lifeguards saying, "Here is the guy I've told you about. Teach him to swim before the week is over." I was stunned, embarrassed, and angry. Edd had betrayed me. He had lied to me. He had tricked me into coming to camp. But by the end of the week, I had learned to swim well enough to earn the swimming merit badge. A couple of weeks later back home, I earned the lifesaving merit badge. In early fall, at a Court of Honor, I became an Eagle Scout along with four of my friends.

Viewed from one angle, I could say that Edd Smart deceived me. But I know better. He didn't deceive me; he believed in me. In fact, he believed in me more than I believed in myself. He was not content to let me stop two merit badges short of Eagle. He risked our friendship, banking on the fact that I could go on and complete the little that I lacked. Even though at the time I appeared to resent him, deep down I think I actually appreciated what he did. I know I appreciate it today. And I never look at my Eagle Scout badge without being thankful for Edd Smart.

We are blessed if we have people in our lives who tell us to keep going. I have had others since scouting days to tell me that at moments when I might have otherwise been tempted to quit, to rest on the memory of past accomplishments, or to look at the future and say, "No way." God has seen fit to put significant people on my path at just the time I needed to hear what they said or needed to do what they counseled. My wife Jeannie is my foremost encourager. But I have also been fortunate to have parents, friends, pastors, and teachers who have been part of my "cheering section." If you have people like this in your life, you need to give thanks for each of them. In fact, it would be appropriate for you to stop right here, turn to the back cover of the book, and write down their names as they come to mind.

In a moment of moving recollection, the apostle Paul remembered the Christians at Philippi. It's likely that this was the first church Paul established in Europe. It was surely the one with whom he formed the strongest bond. Writing back to them from prison years later, he said, "I thank my God every time I remember you . . . because of your sharing in the gospel from the first day until now" (1:3, 5). Other translations use the word "partnership" instead of the word "sharing." I like the idea of partnership. It personalizes it a little more for me, and there's no doubt that Paul felt deep, personal connections to the Christians in Philippi. They had been in his "cheering section" from the very beginning, and the remembrance of that brought the veteran apostle comfort and encouragement from his prison cell. Through thick and thin, the Philippians had told Paul through words and deeds to keep going.

As we come to the last chapter of this book about prayer and devotional life, it can be summed up in two words: Go on! No matter where we are in our faith journey, spiritual formation in the Wesleyan tradition is about continuing . . . about journeying . . . about moving forward into new and deeper experiences of God. John Wesley referred to it as "going on to perfection."[1] This phrase, which sounds strange to our contemporary ears, was actually the heart and soul of early-Methodist devotional life. We cannot bring this book to its appropriate end without seeking to recover this dynamic for ourselves.

Yet we make this quest in an environment that is not always friendly to the effort. The whole idea of "being perfect" turns people off before they even try to understand what Wesley meant by the phrase. And rather than committing ourselves to some open-ended, ever-growing experience of spiritual development, we much prefer a quick-fix approach. "Ninety days to a new you," "six steps to victory," or some other program which awards a certificate of accomplishment at the end is more popular in our world. We like to think of ourselves as "graduates" more than "students on the way." We prefer a terminology of "finding" Jesus, rather than "following him." We opt for plans with arrivals built into them instead of invitations with journeys at their heart.

But if we are to be true to our heritage and, more important, if we are to make that heritage a living and transforming reality for ourselves, we must conclude this book the only way it can end and still be faithful to our tradition. We must follow the counsel of the writer of Hebrews and "consider how to provoke one another to love and good deeds" (10:24). In his now-famous sermon *Catholic Spirit*, Wesley used this verse as the basis for continuing growth in the Christian life, "Provoke me to love and good works. Second thy prayer as thou hast opportunity by speaking to me in love whatsoever thou believest to be for my soul's health. Quicken me in the work which God has given me to do, and instruct me how to do it more perfectly."[2] This is prayer and devotional life for United Methodists.

The best place to begin our recovery is by looking at what is perhaps the major story in the Bible in which a person was tempted to stop. It's the story of the rich man who had a bumper crop, built larger barns to hold the increase, and then said, "Enough" (Luke 12:16-21). Stepping back to consider his assets and accomplishments, he told himself, "Soul, you have ample goods laid up for many years; relax, eat, drink, be merry." But God said to him, "You fool! This very night your life is being demanded of you. And the things you have prepared, whose will they be?"

The parable has layers of meaning, but surely one is that we never come to the place in our spiritual life when we have all we need. Like the wandering Israelites of old, our God-given manna is sufficient only for the day. We cannot store it up or save it for later. Each new moment and each fresh experience calls for its own dispensation of grace. The saints of the ages knew this. We are told that St. Francis of Assisi used to rise to greet the sunrise and exclaim, "Today I begin with God!" How can it be otherwise when we are dealing with an infinite God? We can never come to the end of that relationship or to a moment when we can say, "I don't need anything else." Prayer and devotional life in the Wesleyan tradition is no different. There are always steps to take, dimensions to explore, and experiences to further deepen our walk with God. This is the picture we must see clearly if we are to experience the dynamic of spiritual formation which the Wesleyan tradition holds out for us.

Getting the Picture

When John Wesley exhorted the early Methodists to "go on to perfection," his were not the words of an insatiable tyrant, but rather the encouragement of an incessant lover. Conceiving of God as he did, he could not imagine any point in time or in life when we could cease growing and maturing. And believing in people as he did, he could never be a spiritual guide who counseled them to stay where they were in the life of faith. The only option was to preach, teach, write, sing, and counsel in ways which said, "Keep going!"

But why did he have to use the word "perfect"? I've lost count of the number of times I've been asked a question like that. And I have to admit that on the surface of things, it doesn't seem like the best word to use today. Knowing ourselves and our shortcomings, we can hardly stand to pay attention to something which seems so far fetched—so far beyond any hope of making it a reality. We have all grown up saying and believing, "Nobody's perfect." And even worse, we draw back from those who make overtures in that direction. The idea of Christian perfection strikes us as pretentious. Thus to discover John Wesley making the term a keyword in Methodist spiritual formation is to immediately find ourselves on the horns of a dilemma—namely, how to explore his exhortation without giving way to either caricature or abandonment.

Unfortunately, the history between Wesley's day and ours is strewn with people who went in one direction or the other. On the one hand, we find examples of those who caricatured the idea and ended up with an artificial "perfectionism." Advocates seemed either too good to be true or too driven to be graceful. They appeared to be "too spiritual" for their own good and surely not winsome examples to be emulated. On the other hand, we see those who simply gave up on the idea, either by ignoring it altogether or by saying in effect, "Going on to perfection might have meant something in Wesley's day, but certainly not in ours!" This is often the case in contemporary United Methodism. The result is that Methodism's "grand depositum" has become our forgotten doctrine.[3]

In terms of our theology and the spiritual formation which flows from it, the loss of the idea of Christian perfection is most lamentable. It weakens our doctrine of God, our experience of grace, and the extent to which we can offer transforming hope to those who are pessimistic about themselves and their potential. It leaves us with only the language of behavioral science to describe and deal with issues which wreck the soul and which need a spiritual language to get to the bottom of them. At the same time, however, there is no virtue in reinstating a concept without being led to a sound understanding of it. Unless we can get the picture Wesley hoped to provide, we are no better off. In fact, to revive Christian perfection in ways that create contemporary caricatures will do harm to what we have previously said about prayer and devotional life for United Methodists.

In order to get the picture of what Wesley meant and how we can benefit from it, we must begin by realizing that he was not being unusual or esoteric in encouraging the Methodists to "go on to perfection." The fact that it may strike us that way does not make it so. On the contrary, his call was an attempt to place early-Methodism in the stream of the historic holy-living tradition which had been flowing in the church from its beginning. A consideration of the sources from which he derived his theology of Christian perfection clearly demonstrate that far from being unusual, he was deeply rooted in the teachings and lives of the saints.[4] But what did he actually intend to be the outcome of this rootage?

First, the call to "go on to perfection" was intended to be an encouraging word, not a discouraging one. When we read a quick and contemporary "no-way" response into the theology, we miss it altogether. The call to Christian perfection was seen by Wesley as the supreme invitation to explore and experience the complete potential contained in a theology of grace and a life of discipleship. He called it "the fullness of faith." In one's spiritual life and formation, Wesley could not conceive of any serious devotee being willing to settle for anything short of that. Put simply, why would any of us want to stop with being 70 percent committed or 90 percent righteous? While realizing our performance is never 100 percent correct 100 percent of the time, shouldn't *our heart's desire* be to that end? Isn't the motivation of prayer and devotional life to be totally devoted to God? Wesley surely saw it this way, and in order to keep the motivation alive, he used a term which always calls us to move forward in faith.

This is easy to see when we view it the other way around. Suppose for a moment that we could have a concept of 80 percent righteousness. What would it do to us? Most likely, it would create an instant and artificial sense that we had arrived. Most of us would find some way to convince ourselves that—

despite our faults and failures—we were probably 80 percent of the way there. And since we had already agreed that 80 percent is good enough, the motivation to improve would be seriously undercut. We would be exactly at the point where the man in the parable was; we would find ourselves saying, "Soul, rest and take your ease, you have all you need."

But it's even worse than that. What about the remaining 20 percent? Since we had already agreed that 80 percent was adequate, we would surely find ways to justify the 20 percent of our lives which were unaffected by the gospel. We would be award-winning rationalizers, with a built-in concept to justify our lack of repentance or the desire to make right what was still obviously wrong. The only way to avoid these pitfalls is to say, "Go on to perfection." Far from being a message of neurosis, it is a message of motivation. Rather than being a word aimed to discourage us, it is one intended to let us know that we never have to give up and say, "This is it. This is all I ever can be." No, the call to "go on to perfection" is the invitation to remain open and responsive to new experiences of healing, reconciling, and empowering grace.

Second, the call to "go on to perfection" was a great protection against pride. The fact that you and I say, "Well, I'll tell you one thing for sure—I'm not perfect," is a major means to keep us from ever thinking that we are! The immediate response some people had to the idea of Christian perfection was, in fact, the response Wesley wanted people to have! He had seen people who professed to be tee-totally perfect and witnessed the devastating effects such presumption had on their attitudes and actions. He abhorred any construction of the Christian faith that had an "arrival" mentality. By connecting early Methodism with the holy-living tradition of Christian perfection, he was doing his best to keep it from deteriorating into a museum of self-satisfied disciples. If the term "perfection" troubled some of his followers, or troubles us today, it was meant to! He wanted us to have such a grand view of Christian growth that we would never rest content in any single experience, allowing that experience to become a "dead center."

I majored in Sociology in college. The older I get, the more insights this major brings to my Christian faith and life. Sociologists have a term called "ethnocentrism." It is the belief that your group is superior to other groups. It is the feeling that you have it made—especially in relation to others. Eighteenth-century England was still giddy with what some have called "the gilded age." All sorts of manners and customs were used to show how one level of society was finer than another. Lines of demarcation were clearly drawn. Wesley, and others who viewed faith and life similarly to him, was convinced that pride was one of the main enemies to be dealt with. The doctrine of Christian perfection was one means by which to do it. Whether king or commoner, no one could claim to have "made it," to have "arrived," or to be "above" anyone else. Regardless of class, status, success, security, or wealth, everyone was involved in the same spiritual journey. Everyone could advance in the love of God and the love of neighbor.

Third, the call to "go on to perfection" meant that the present moment was more valuable than any moment in the past—more central than any moment in the future. I believe, for example, that this is why he did not dwell on his Aldersgate experience of 1738. Some have viewed his relative disinterest as a sign that it didn't matter that much to him, but the references that he does make to it show it to be very important. Instead, his reluctance to make his heart-warming experience on May 24th the "be all and end all" lies precisely in his call to Christian perfection. The present moment is the divine moment. Any retreat to the past—or worse, a resting upon the past—does damage to the spiritual life. Likewise, projecting toward a future which does not exist only undercuts and delays spiritual progress which should be occurring now. The only valid option is "going on...."

Fourth, the call to "go on to perfection" was the invitation to experience the depths of grace. We have repeatedly seen in this book that a theology of grace is the basis for spiritual formation in the Wesleyan tradition. Prayer and devotional life is a way of describing our response to grace and our lifelong participation in it. The apostle John wrote these words in his gospel about Christ and our life in him: "From his fullness we have all received grace upon grace" (1:16). We cannot cease our experience of grace any more than we can stop the tides! Yes, we can get in our cars and drive away from the ocean. We can take some snapshots of our trip to the beach and relive it when looking through our photo albums. But these are paltry options compared to letting one wave after another wash over us. We can back away from God's "waves of grace." We can take a few theological pictures and stare at them the rest of our lives, but to do so will be to miss the very experience of grace God intends for us.

We must get the picture Wesley was trying to paint. We must not allow one word to throw us off course, thus missing the heart of prayer and devotional life. The four concepts outlined above are not the whole story, but they point us in the right direction. They encourage us rather than discourage us. They point us away from pride and presumption. They keep the Christian life from having a point where we can "arrive" and then "retire." They save us from staring at a few "photos" of the spiritual life when the real thing is much more like a video tape that is being made day after day.

I have always been moved by the testimony of E. Stanley Jones when he was asked to name the best years of his life. He always said, "The next ten." He got the picture, and he was living it out in a forward-looking, dynamic discipleship. His prayer and devotional life was the ongoing evidence that he knew what the heart of the Christian life was all about—

unceasing devotion to God through Christ in the power of the Spirit. A proper view of Christian perfection resulted in a dynamic discipleship which made the decade to come as meaningful as any he had experienced. And even after a debilitating stroke from which he never recovered, Stanley Jones could write that everything he believed and preached about the Christian life was true!

We cannot leave this section without connecting what Wesley was attempting to do in the eighteenth century with contemporary spiritual formation. E. Stanley Jones is one person in the twentieth century who helped us get the picture. But the bridge which connected Wesley's time and ours is much longer than the testimony of one person. The nineteenth century and the ongoing flow of the holy-living tradition into the present connects us with a heritage of people who have given similar witness. In the helpful story of United Methodism in America given by editor John G. McEllhenney in the book *Proclaiming Grace and Freedom*, the point is succinct and clear, "It is significant that Methodists, United Brethren, and Evangelicals all emphasized the doctrine of justification by faith alone and Christian perfection."[5] This brief sentence shows how United Methodism today is the inheritor of multiple streams in which the call to "go on to perfection" has gone forth. Frederick Norwood further expanded the view by showing how a renewed interest in holiness became a central feature in the nineteenth century through the revival movement and the establishment of denominations like the Wesleyan Church and the Free Methodist Church.[6] Similar commitments to the holy-living tradition can be seen in later denominations such as the Assemblies of God and the Church of the Nazarene.

This historical citation is not intended to merely record institutional data, but rather to show that what we are pointing to in this chapter is within the core of United Methodism and some of the sister denominations that have come out of it, or grown up alongside it. The picture of holiness of heart and life which pervades this book is not a "back-water" detour from a more central message—-it is the essence of the message. It is the theological food which produces the fruit of authentic prayer and devotional life. If we must acknowledge our ignorance of this heritage and spend time reacquainting ourselves with it, let's do it! If we must confess our caricatured reactions and move beyond them to a proper view of the doctrine, so be it! But most of all, we must know that when it comes to spiritual formation in general, or prayer and devotional life in particular, the call is focused and singular: Go on! And having seen this, we must now explore some of the implications of what this commitment means.

Embracing the Reality

Holiness of heart and life is connected to our theology of grace—sanctifying grace in particular. Because "going on to perfection" is ultimately a life to be lived more than a doctrine to be studied, we must view it in relation to the means of grace which we have earlier examined. In this final section we want to concentrate on prayer—the chief instituted means of grace. We want to see how prayer helps convey sanctifying grace to us. We want to see how it fits into our larger devotional life as an overall means to growing in grace.

First, prayer is the means of discovering the pattern for ongoing growth. The pattern which enables us to "go on to perfection" is most profoundly described by Jesus in John 15. Christian spiritual formation is ultimately nothing other than abiding in Christ. Using the analogy of the vine and branch, we learn that we are made for growth. Jesus called it "bearing much fruit." Abiding in Christ is the means to effect the growth. Our fruit is the result of our prior and ongoing relationship with the Master.

John 15 also describes how that growth is to occur. Dr. David McKenna has called it the "reproductive cycle."[7] Through Jesus' words, Dr. McKenna sees the natural process of planting the roots, growing the vine, pruning the branches, and harvesting the fruit. But the natural process is analogous to the spiritual-formation process intended for all disciples: growing down (roots), giving up (to the vine), cutting back (the branches), and letting go (producing the fruit). McKenna calls this the "Christ cycle" of spiritual growth.

John 15 was one of John Wesley's favorite passages in the Bible. It was the text used at the annual covenant-renewal services. In his *Explanatory Notes Upon the New Testament*, Wesley connected "abiding in Christ" to prayer.[8] This is surely because he understood the essence of the Christian life to be a living relationship with God. Relationships are begun and sustained with communication between the parties. Prayer is the "grand means" for nurturing that relationship. Just as a vine is nurtured by the branch it is connected to, so our spirits are strengthened as we commune with God in prayer. This core chapter in John's gospel evokes a prayer life through which we ask practical, nurturing questions such as these:

"Where do I need to more strongly attach myself to Christ?"

"Have I given Christ permission to indwell me completely?"

"What fruit is my relationship with Christ producing?"

"Are there areas in my life that need pruning?"

Prayer produces a harvest of insights, just as Wesley said, and the insights evoke new questions which, in turn, yield additional discoveries.

Over the years, I have discovered the increasing value of using prayer-questions in my devotional life. Prayer-questions specify the issues. Like Velcro, they give something specific for God to "stick" answers and insights to. They reveal the desires of my heart. They help shape the thoughts of my mind. They help chart the course of my actions. I like to set a specific passage of scripture in front of me and then begin to ask as many questions as I can about it—especially questions that bring the external Word to internal relevance. This kind of prayer enables me to see the larger pattern for "going on to perfection" as it unfolds over time.

In our attempt to keep all this as practical as possible, let me suggest five prayer questions which can open the pages of the Bible in new ways and can result in deep periods of contemplation with God:

1. *What does this passage say?* This is the question which enables us to observe the text itself. It can prevent us from reading things into the text which are not there. It keeps us focused on the main words and ideas of the passage.

2. *What does the passage mean?* Here we prayerfully consider the interpretations which naturally emerge from the passage and our reflection upon it.

3. *How does this passage connect with other passages and other meaningful literature?* This question helps us correlate the text with other Bible passages, hymns, sermons, and other devotional material which has influenced us. This question helps us connect the text to related elements in our formation.

4. *Where is the value in this passage for me right now?* This question helps us evaluate the significance of the text for our   growth in grace in the present moment. Not every verse is equally valuable all the time. We are looking for that "pearl of great price," so we look for the value each passage has for us at the time we are reading it.

5. *What must I do about what I have read?* This is the application question which transforms theory into practice—

abstractions into actions—resolutions into realities. This final question, asked in a time of prayerful devotion keeps holiness of heart and holiness of life together, creating the natural outflow of inspired intake.[9]

You may find this combination of prayer and study to be awkward at first, but keep using it until it becomes natural. I have been studying the Bible this way for more than twenty-five years. It has become the place where prayer and Bible reading are joined into a living whole. It is the experience by which the written word becomes the living word. Prayer questions open us to the power of the passage.

Second, prayer provides the guidance for us to pursue the vision. Abiding in Christ is a big subject, with multiplied expressions and ramifications throughout the Bible, to say nothing of all the other formative literature in which the subject is found. Prayer and devotional life helps us quiet our spirit in relation to all the possibilities and zero-in on a few particulars which emerge from contemplation. It is not possible to be holy "all over the map" all at once. Prayer enables us to concentrate on selected concrete realities. Prayer is like the channel selector on the remote control, guiding us "program by program" through all the options and giving us the opportunity to click on the dimensions of spiritual growth that are most important at the time.

For years now, I have prayed this question, "God, what would you have me to be doing at this time in my life to grow in your grace?" Each segment of the question gives shape to my spiritual formation. To say "God" is to acknowledge the Source for my growth in grace. To ask "what" is to remember that I am not called by God to be growing simultaneously in every area. God is gracious, revealing a few items for special consideration. To use the word "me" is to recall that my going on to perfection is not identical with someone else's. There is an agenda and process tailored to my unique personhood and needs. Including the phrase "to be doing" reminds me that I am not a passive observer, waiting for God to dump something on me. Rather, I am called to respond in concrete ways to the waves of grace which wash up on the shore of my soul. "At this time in my life" is a phrase that applies God's grace to the present moments of my life, assuring me that my age, stage, and circumstances are part of my spiritual life—that spiritual formation occurs in the realities of my everyday existence. And finally, to say the words "to grow in your grace" is to speak the goal of it all. I am not practicing prayer and devotional life for any other reason. There may be many benefits, but only one purpose. This prayer question sets the stage for receptivity, enabling me to realize that the primary word is not what I have to say to God, but rather what God wants to say to me.

E. Stanley Jones spoke of his daily quiet time as "going to the Listening Post."[10] I am fortunate to have a picture of Brother Stanley taken during one of his morning devotions while on a trip to Korea. He has risen early and found a relaxed place where he can sit with his open Bible, notebook, and watch on the table. With pen in hand, he is waiting to capture any insights which God might choose to give. It is only a snapshot of a split second in E. Stanley Jones' life, but it is really a visual symbol of the kind of person he was day after day for decades. Like so many others, he understood that one of the chief values in prayer was its ability to serve as a vehicle for God to use in guiding us. He described the guiding process as moving from one stage to another—beginning with a quiet heart, which becomes quiet confidence, which becomes quiet power.[11]

We must not underestimate the importance of this kind of praying. Nor must we leave it to chance. Praying which results in guidance is no vague thing. It is expressed in specific times, places, and ways. I have found the following suggestions from E. Stanley Jones to be especially helpful, and I offer them to you as you move farther into the life of prayer. As you practice them, you will make your own adaptations and improvements, but this model contains some of the main ingredients in a devotional life designed to help us "go on to perfection":

1. Decide on the amount of time you can give to the quiet time, preferably in the morning. The morning is best—it tunes your instrument for the day.
2. Having fixed the time, stick to it. Pray by the clock, whether or not you feel like it.
3. Take your Bible and read a portion slowly. Let it soak in. If some verse strikes you, let your mind circle around it in meditation. It will render up new meanings to you. Write them in a notebook or on the margin of your Bible.
4. After the reading, let go and relax and say to [God], "Father, have you anything to say to me?" Begin to listen. Become guidable.
5. Then you say to God what you have to say. Prayer is dialogue, not monologue.
6. Thank [God] for the answer. He always answers "Yes" or "No." "No" is an answer as well as "Yes"—sometimes a better answer. The answer sometimes may be in you—you are better for having prayed—you are the answer. In the quiet time you become the focal point of transmission for transformation.[12]

I especially like the phrase "the focal point of transmission for transformation." God guides us in prayer in order that we might be personally transformed. In turn, God calls us to be agents of transformation for others. There is hardly a better way to describe holiness of heart and life, and prayer is the means by which it happens in our lives.

Third, prayer is the means of balancing contemplation and action. Douglas Steere, one of my favorite writers on prayer, states it clearly, "Contemplation is not a state of coma or of religious reverie. If it is genuine prayer, we find our inward life quickened. We sense new directions, or our attention is refocused on neglected ones. We find ourselves being mobilized and our inward resources regrouped to the new assignment."[13] Far from the caricature which says that prayer is detachment from real life, the testimony of Steere and so many others like him is that it is the seedbed out of which inspired action comes.

At this point we are dropped right back into the heart of John 15. Jesus said, "Apart from me you can do nothing." Abiding in Christ is the means to connect intention with fulfillment. Henri Nouwen said it this way, "Dwelling in Christ is what prayer is all about."[14] It is this praying which enables Christ to give us his eyes to see the world, his ears to hear the cries of those around us, and his heart to do what we can rather than opting out or expecting that someone else will act. Prayer is the means through which we enlist ourselves in Christ's mission in the world.

This does not have to be a complicated commitment. In fact, one of the things I've discovered is how our predecessors in faith came to deep experiences of powerful simplicity. The following comments by Mother Teresa reveal the combination of contemplation and action, expressed in simple phrases:

> Let us all become a true and faithful branch on the vine
> Jesus, by accepting Him in our lives as it pleases Him
> to come:
> >   as the Truth—to be told;
> >   as the Life—to be lived;
> >   as the Light—to be lighted;
> >   as the Love—to be loved;
> >   as the Way—to be walked;
> >   as the Joy—to be given;
> >   as the Peace—to be spread;
> >   as the Sacrifice—to be offered;
> in our families and within our neighborhoods.[15]

I do not know of any words which better convey the substance and spirit of Wesley's emphasis upon holiness of heart and life. The connection between contemplation and action is so natural in Mother Teresa's counsel that we can hardly tell where one ends and the other begins. That's the way it should be—a seamless connection between the quality of our inner life and the ministry of our outer living.

Fourth, we must hasten to say that prayer is the means of receiving the power to live the life we so passionately want to live. If apart from Christ we can do nothing, then in Christ we can do all things! How tragic it would be to have eyes to see and ears to hear, but to be impotent to act. Abiding in Christ is the means to receive the power to do what our hearts tell us to do. This power is given only in relation to a deep sense of dependence upon Jesus. We do not go far down the road of holy living before we realize it is a supernatural task. And supernatural tasks require supernatural power.

I recently attended a simulcast of the "Purpose Driven Church" conference, conducted by Rick Warren, senior pastor of Saddleback Church in Mission Viejo, California. Like so many others, I had heard about his congregation and the effective ways he was discovering to move them along in the life of discipleship.[16] I joined over 30,000 others in 75 cities by means of satellite technology. Midway through the day, Rick interviewed Max Lucado, senior pastor at Oak Hills Church of Christ in San Antonio, Texas. Max has recently led the congregation in adopting the purpose-driven concept. As he described the almost three years that Oak Hills spent in making the transition, more than once he noted the role of prayer in the process. It was prayer which gave rise to the vision to move in that direction. Prayer preceded the actual launch of the new paradigm, and prayer was continuing to undergird the journey. God challenged the Oak Hills congregation with a supernatural task; it required supernatural power to achieve it.

At the risk of sounding like someone using old cliches, I want to make it clear: I am convinced that individual Christians and corporate congregations must experience renewal in prayer if they are to discover the power to be who God calls them to be and to do what God calls them to do. We need this more than any other single thing. We have spent too much time trying to catch visions, discover gifts, motivate people, train leaders, achieve unity, and carry out our mission—*in our own strength*. I know plenty of congregations that pray for God to bless their plans, and thankfully God is gracious and does so a lot of the time. But what we need is more congregations who will pray for God to give them their plans! The same holds true for our individual discipleship. When God is the author of the vision, power accompanies the revelation.

When you opened this book and began to read the introduction, I told you that I was writing differently now than I might have a few years ago. I emphasized that this was not merely a book to inform you but also one to inspire you! We are now at the heart of that inspiration—going on to perfection. Prayer and devotional life for United Methodists— indeed, for all Christians—is nothing other than the lifelong response to grace as we abide in Christ and he indwells us. What we have seen in the pages of this book is not a plan, but a Person—the risen Christ, who longs to have fellowship with us on a continuous journey marked by specific periods of prayer and devotion.

When John Wesley lay dying in his house in London, friends gathered around the old man. What could he tell them as he made the transition from earth to heaven? What words could he speak to encourage and strengthen them? Was there some word to sum it up? Yes, there was. And one of the last things they ever heard him say was this: "The best of all is, God is with us." You cannot improve on that. It is prayer and devotional life for United Methodists.

Living It Out

1. What part of the chapter did God use to speak the clearest word to you? Why is this an important message for you right now? Take a few moments to write down some specific ways you can take this message and activate it in your life.
2. Before you read this chapter, had you ever heard the phrase, "going on to perfection"? If so, what did you think of it? Did this chapter help you see what it means in a more positive light? How? If you were forced not to use the word "perfection" in communicating this idea to someone else, what word or phrase would you choose in its place?
3. Take your favorite Bible passage and for the next five days use one of the prayer questions on page 100 each day to create a prayerful reading of the text.
4. Take Mother Teresa's prayer on page 105. Select any two of her application phrases (e.g., a "Truth—to be told") and think of one specific action you could take to make the idea a part of your life situation.
5. You have come to the end of this book. Review it briefly and then write out a short paragraph summarizing the major effect it has had on your life. Do not ignore particular struggles it may have caused. This can also be part of your spiritual formation. Simply capture several abiding values which have been yours as you have read, reflected upon, and shared this book with others in your group.

Appendix A

Covenant Prayer

THE FORMATION OF community in the Wesleyan tradition is connected to the act of covenant making. When we gather in groups for edifying fellowship, we should form our fellowship through a covenant. One way to do this is to pray the following prayer:

Leader: God is a covenant-making God. Through the everlasting covenant God has promised to be our God, and we are invited to be God's people. This group experience provides us the opportunity to renew our covenant with God and with one another. As we begin our time together, let us yield anew ourselves to God.

People: **I am no longer my own, but Yours. Put me to what You will, rank me with whom You will; put me to doing, put me to suffering; let me be employed for You or laid aside for You, exalted for You or brought low for You; let me be full, let me be empty; let me have all things, let me have nothing; I freely and heartily yield all things to Your pleasure and disposal. And now, O glorious and blessed God, Father, Son and Holy Spirit, You are mine, and I am Yours. So be it. And the covenant which I have made on earth, let it be ratified in heaven. Amen.****

Appendices

> Leader: In the spirit of that prayer and in the assurance that God receives our dedication, let us commit ourselves to one another and to a fruitful use of our time together.

* Note: This prayer has been part of the traditional Covenant Renewal Service used in Methodism prior to the establishment of The United Methodist Church. The prayer is an adaptation of the original spirit and prayers which John Wesley used with the early-Methodists.

Appendix B

Praying Together

IN ADDITION TO the Covenant Prayer, your group should experience other times of prayer together. The following options are suggested as means to enrich the praying you do in your weekly sessions.

1 It's always appropriate to incorporate the Lord's Prayer at whatever point in the session you choose. Groups often use the Lord's Prayer as a means to conclude the meeting.

2. Ask group members to bring their favorite prayer to the next meeting. At prayer time, have each person read the selected prayer out loud.

3. Some people in the group may be new and nervous when it comes to praying out loud spontaneously. Have several books of prayers available and invite people to select a prayer to share during the prayer time.

4. Ask group members to bring an article from the newspaper that moved them to pray. At the prayer time, have each person share the selected article, and at the end of each person's sharing, let the group pray, "Lord, be at work in this situation for Your glory and for the good of those involved."

5. Ask group members to bring photographs of family members for whom they are praying. At the prayer time, have each person hold up the photograph, name the person, and share why they are praying for that person right now. At the end of each person's sharing, let the group pray, "Lord, in your mercy, hear our prayer for *(the person's name)*."

6. Experiment with one-word prayer. At the prayer time, the leader asks each group member to select one "prayer word" which expresses a feeling or a desire. Have each person speak that word aloud, allowing for quiet pauses between each expression.

7. Ask group members to write down the names of the people they most want to pray for right now (e.g., neighbors, family members, work associates, etc.), and beside each name a one-word intercession (e.g., "Jim—for healing"). At the prayer time, let each person read his or her list.

8. At one of your sessions, pray for the church. Begin with your group, then move along to your Sunday school class, your pastor and lay leaders, the district superintendent, the bishop, the annual conference, and the larger United Methodist Church. As you are able, pray specifically and by name in relation to these facets of the church.

Appendix C

A Mini-Retreat

A GROWING NUMBER of persons are practicing personal and group retreat. You may wish to bring your reading and reflection of this book to a close in this manner. The following model for a half-day retreat is designed with a small group in mind, but it can easily be adapted to a personal retreat. The times in parentheses are merely illustrative to give you a sense of the flow for the retreat experience.

For this retreat you will need to have on hand this book, your Bible, a copy of *The United Methodist Hymnal* (or other hymnal in sufficient quantities for all group members), and a journal to record insights that come during the retreat itself. If possible, also have someone at the retreat who can play guitar or other instrument to lead you in music.

Arrival (9:00-9:30 a.m.)
Let this be a time for 'settling in' to your surroundings. Greet one another, but pay particular attention to the environment in which your retreat will take place. For the most part, this should be about a half-hour of silence. You may wish to take a brief walk around the area where you'll be meeting. Regardless of what you do, thank God for these hours, your retreat place, others who are joining you, and for the opportunity to bring your reading of this book to this kind of closure.

Appendices

Community Singing (9:30-9:45 a.m.)
Your worship leader will break the silence by singing a capella the first verse of a hymn or chorus. Everyone listens quietly while the verse is sung, and then together the entire group will repeat the first stanza. After that, the worship leader will move through approximately fifteen minutes of community singing. Use hymns and choruses which reflect the themes you have encountered in the book.

Community Prayer (9:45-10:00 a.m.)
For the next fifteen minutes, pray together. By now, your group will have found certain prayer styles to be meaningful and comfortable. Use them in this section of the retreat. Emphasize a spirit of gratitude to God for those things which come to mind during this season of prayer. Let the worship leader close this segment by inviting everyone to pray the Lord's Prayer.

"The Treasure Hidden in the Field" (10:00-10:30 a.m.)
Your leader will now invite you to get some distance between yourselves, so you can experience a half-hour of personal devotional time. Let the first ten minutes or so be a time to quiet down and just enjoy your surroundings. Let the second ten minutes be a time to meditate on this question, "If someone asked me how I have grown closer to Christ through the use of this book, what would I say?" Use the final ten minutes to write down your response and to consider how you might wish to share this with the other members of your group.

A Time of Refreshment (10:30-10:45 a.m.)
Regather around light refreshments, and enjoy visiting informally for fifteen minutes with other members in your group.

Overflowing Hearts (10:45-11:15 a.m.)
Move into the group segment of the retreat by singing together a selected hymn or chorus. Then allow a relaxed half-hour of sharing the "treasure" you found during your personal devotional times.

Continuing the Journey (11:15-11:30 a.m.)
Transition the group-sharing into a time for your group to consider where God may be leading toward the next step in the journey. Your goal in this fifteen minutes is not to decide anything, but rather to listen as group members share where they sense God may be wanting them to go. There is no pressure to pick anything for this group to do next. In fact, the group itself may disband. This segment is merely to verbalize possible directions and to see how God leads from there.

Gathering at the Table (11:30 a.m.-12:00 noon)
If you are using *The United Methodist Hymnal,* turn to the Service of Word and Table II (pp. 12-15). Bring your retreat time to closure through the celebration of the Lord's Supper.

Appendix D

What Now?

I_F YOUR EXPERIENCE using this resource was positive, you can expect some "let down" now that the study is concluded. You may miss the regular reading and reflection as well as the weekly interaction with group members. If your experience was negative or if it has created struggle in your soul, you may be tempted to shelve this book and be done with it. Feelings like these are entirely natural. The important thing is to know how to process your experience in the best possible way. Whether positive or negative, or somewhere in between, it has been a time to think about prayer and devotional life with particular focus.

Now what?

(1) Let things soak for about a week to ten days. Like seeds sown in the ground, your impressions and experiences need time to make the transition from the short-term to the long-term. For a while, don't go back and try to re-do anything, second-guess anything, or improve anything. Just let things "be." Trust that the Holy Spirit is at work to use this experience for your good and God's glory.

(2) After a couple of weeks have passed, revisit your overall impressions. Have they changed in any way?

Appendices

Are they clearer? Have new ideas or feelings attached to them? Now that you have some distance from the actual use of the material, what do you think God is saying to you now?

(3) If you formed any good friendships in your group, this may be a good time to share with one or two others, to see what is emerging in their lives as a result of their time in this book.

(4) As you process the long-term results, keep your reflection and your decisions in the context of the two major categories set forth in chapter one: communion and compassion. What signs of growth and/or "marching orders" for the future are you sensing as you move on in your discipleship?

(5) About a month after you complete this study, take your emerging observations and see if there are any resources in Appendix E which may be especially helpful to keep the growth pattern moving along. If nothing strikes you, but you feel the importance of continuing your study and formation, talk with your pastor or the manager of a good Christian bookstore for suggestions.

(6) See if any of the other volumes in the "Life Enriching Practices" series are where God would have you go next. More than anything else, remain confident that God is at work in your life.

Appendix E

For Further Study

THE FOLLOWING RESOURCES are recommended to enable you to go farther in your study of a particular aspect of this book. The first two sections contain general resources akin to the overall theme of the book. Subsequent sections contain resources for the sectional themes. In addition to these recommendations, pay attention to the endnotes for works which are specifically related to particular ideas in the book.

General Resources in Wesleyan Spirituality

Gregory S. Clapper, *As If the Heart Mattered: A Wesleyan Spirituality* (Nashville: Upper Room Books, 1997).

Kenneth J. Collins, *The Scripture Way of Salvation: The Heart of John Wesley's Theology* (Nashville: Abingdon Press, 1998).

Donald E. Demaray, ed., *The Daily Wesley* (Anderson, Ind.: Bristol House, 1994).

Donald E. Demaray, ed., *Wesley's Daily Prayers* (Anderson, Ind.: Briston House, 1998).

Steve Harper, *Devotional Life in the Wesleyan Tradition: A Workbook* (Nashville: Upper Room Books, 1995).

Steve Harper, *John Wesley's Message for Today* (Grand Rapids, Mich.: Zondervan Publishing House, 1983).

Russell D. Jeffrey, *A Window of Grace: Wesleyan Insights on Effective Prayer* (Indianapolis, Ind.: Light and Life Communications, 1997).

Rueben P. Job, *A Wesleyan Spiritual Reader* (Nashville: Abingdon Press, 1997).

Henry H. Knight, III, *The Presence of God in the Christian Life: John Wesley And the Means of Grace* (Metuchen, N.J.: The Scarecrow Press, 1992).

Theodore Runyon, *The New Creation: John Wesley's Theology Today* (Nashville: Abingdon Press, 1998).

General Resources in Spiritual Formation

M. Robert Mulholland, Jr., *Invitation to a Journey* (Downers Grove, Ill.: InterVarsity Press, 1993).

Susan Annette Muto, *Pathways to Spiritual Living* (St. Bede's, 1984).

Henri Nouwen, *Making All Things New: An Invitation to the Spiritual Life* (San Francisco: Harper & Row, 1981).

Marjorie J. Thompson, *Soul Feast: An Invitation to the Christian Spiritual Life* (Louisville: Westminster John Knox Press, 1995).

Wesley Tracy et al., *The Upward Call* (Kansas City: Beacon Hill Press, 1994).

Evelyn Underhill, *The Spiritual Life* (San Francisco: Harper & Row).

Communion

Thomas Kelly, *A Testament of Devotion* (New York: Harper and Row, 1941).

Henri Nouwen, *The Way of the Heart* (New York: Seabury Press, 1981).

Charles R. Swindoll, *Intimacy With the Almighty* (Dallas: Word, 1996).

Evelyn Underhill, *The House of the Soul* (New York: Seabury Press, 1984).

Appendices

Compassion

Richard Foster, *Streams of Living Water,* chapter five, "The Social Justice Tradition: Discovering the Compassionate Life" (San Francisco: Harper Collins, 1998).

Henri Nouwen et al., *Compassion: A Reflection on the Christian Life* (New York: Doubleday Image Books, 1983).

John Michael Talbot, *The Lessons of St. Francis*, chapter nine, "Compassion"(New York: Penguin Plume Book, 1997).

Classical Formation

Richard Foster, *Streams of Living Water* (cited above)
Also see the entries under the section "General Resources in Spiritual Formation."

Concrete Structures

Thomas E. Frank, *Polity, Practice, and the Mission of The United Methodist Church* (Nashville: Abingdon Press, 1997).

Russell E. Richey et al, *Connectionalism: Ecclesiology, Mission, and Identity*, Volume 1 in the "United Methodism and American Culture" series (Nashville: Abingdon Press, 1997).

Howard A. Snyder, *The Radical Wesley and Patterns for Church Renewal* (Grand Rapids: Francis Asbury Press, 1980).

Jack M. Tuell, *The Organization of The United Methodist Church: 1997-2000 Edition* (Nashville: Abingdon Press, 1997).

Formative Reading

M. Robert Mulholland, Jr., *Shaped by the Word* (Nashville: Upper Room Books, 1985).

David L. Thompson, *Bible Study That Works* (Nappanee, Ind.: Evangel Press, 1994).

Robert L. Traina, *Methodical Bible Study* (Grand Rapids: Zondervan, 1985).

Walter Wink, *Transforming Bible Study* (Nashville: Abingdon Press, 1990).

Prayer

Roberta C. Bondi, *A Place to Pray: Reflections on the Lord's Prayer* (Nashville: Abingdon Press, 1998). Dr. Bondi has also produced a seven-part video series by the same title, likewise available from Abingdon Press.

O. Richard Bowye et al. *Prayer in the Black Tradition* (Nashville: Upper Room Books, 1986).

Richard Foster, *Prayer: Finding the Heart's True Home* (San Francisco: Harper Collins, 1992).

E. Dee Freeborn, *When You Pray: Going Everywhere with Jesus* (Kansas City: Beacon Hill Press, 1992).

Timothy Jones, *The Art of Prayer: A Simple Guide* (New York: Ballantine Books, 1997).

Douglas V. Steere, *Dimensions of Prayer* (Nashville: Upper Room Books, 1997).

Terry Teykll, *Pray the Price: United Methodists United in Prayer* (Muncie, Ind.: Prayer Point Press, 1997).

Also see the resources under the section entitled "Communion."

Getting the Picture

Andrew Murray, *Holy in Christ* (Minneapolis: Bethany Fellowship).

W.E. Stangster, *The Path to Perfection* (London: Epworth Press, 1984).

Mack B. Stokes, *The Holy Spirit in the Wesleyan Heritage* (Nashville: Abingdon Press, 1985).

Charles Yrigoyen, Jr., *John Wesley: Holiness of Heart and Life* (Nashville: Abingdon Press, 1999).

Appendices

Embracing the Reality

Maxie Dunnam, *The Workbook on Becoming Alive in Christ* (Nashville: Upper Room Books, 1989).

David L. McKenna, *Growing Up in Christ* (Indianapolis: Light and Life Communications, 1998).

E. Stanley Jones, *Christian Maturity* (Nashville: Abingdon Press, 1957).

Notes

Notes to Chapter 1

1. Richard Foster, *Celebration of Discipline* (San Francisco: Harper & Row, 1978), 1.
2. Gregory S. Clapper, *As If The Heart Mattered* (Nashville: Upper Room Books, 1997). This excellent work succinctly describes the relationship between "heart religion" and the Wesleyan tradition.
3. Benedicta Ward, *The Sayings of the Desert Fathers* (London & Oxford: Mowbrays, 1975), 8.
4. BW, Vol. 9, 69.
5. BW, Vol. 9, 70.
6. BW, Vol. 9, 72.
7. For an excellent treatment of Wesley's theology of Christian experience, see Theodore Runyon's *The New Creation: John Wesley's Theology Today* (Nashville: Abingdon Press, 1998), chapter 5.
8. Frederick Norwood, *The Story of American Methodism* (Nashville: Abingdon Press, 1974), 112.
9. BW, Vol. 1, 131-141; "The Almost Christian."
10. Peter Canisius and Johannes Van Lierde, eds., *Prayers and Devotions from Pope John Paul II,* (New York: Viking, 1994), 56.
11. JW, Vol. 14, 32.
12. Runyon, *The New Creation*, 163.
13. BW, Vol. 4, 174.
14. Karl Barth, *Church Dogmatics*, Vol. IV/1 (Edinburgh: T & T Clark, 1956), 190.
15. For an extended treatment of compassion using this threefold pattern, see Henri Nouwen, Donald P. McNeill, and Douglas A. Morrison, *Compassion: A Reflection on the Christian Life* (New York: Image Books, Doubleday, 1982).
16. I have given additional treatment to the means of grace in my book, *Devotional Life in the Wesleyan Tradition* (Nashville: Upper Room Books, 1983) and in its revision, *Devotional Life in the Wesleyan Tradition: A Workbook* (Nashville: Upper Room Books, 1995).

17. BW, Vol. 1, 380.
18. It is important to see this connection to further root this view in the larger Christian tradition. Wesley, however, avoided making direct reference to Roman Catholicism, lest the means of grace be thrown out by those with anti-Catholic sentiments. The phrase "means of grace" was a way of communicating truth to those who would otherwise not have paid attention to it.
19. BW, Vol. 1, 387.
20. The prudential means are detailed in *The Nature, Design, and General Rules of The United Societies,* which Wesley published in 1743 to guide the early-Methodists in their life together and their service for Christ in daily living. See BW, Vol. 9, 69-75.
21. BW, Vol. 3, 208.

Notes to Chapter 2

1. TL, Vol. 4, 103
2. BW, Vol. 19, 29
3. The phrase "the life of God in the soul of man" is often attributed to Henry Scougal, a 17th century Scottish devotional writer and professor of divinity. But others, including John Wesley, used the phrase to describe the essence of the spiritual life.
4. The Lover-beloved concept is a beautiful metaphor for the devotional life. Bernard of Clairvaux, Clare of Assisi, and Francis of Assisi helped establish it in Christian spirituality. John Michael Talbor (*The Lover and the Beloved,* 1988) and Henri Nouwen (*Life of the Beloved,* 1992) have perpetuated the concept for contemporary readers.
5. Sociologist Robert Wuthnow documents major shifts in spirituality in his book, *After Heaven: Spirituality in America Since the 1950's* (Berkeley, CA: University of California Press, 1998).
6. Susan Muto, *Pathways of Spiritual Living* (Garden City, NY: Doubleday Image Book, 1984), 77. This book was subsequently reprinted by St. Bede's Publications in 1988.
7. M. Robert Mulholland Jr., *Invitation to a Journey* (Downers Grove, IL: InterVarsity Press, 1993), 113.
8. SOSO, vi.
9. EOT, Vol. 1, ix. He repeated this same counsel in JW, Vol. 14, 253.
10. JW, Vol. 14, 217.
11. Mulholland, *Invitation to a Journey,* 114.
12. JW, Vol. 11, 261 and Vol. 14, 217.
13. ENT, 9. Wesley agreed with Luther to the extent that he used this quotation in the Preface to *Explanatory Notes Upon the New Testament,* which he published in 1755.

14. *Dr. Martin Luther's Works*, the standard edition commonly known as the Weimar Ausgabe edition (WA), published in 55 volumes beginning in 1957, "A Right Way to Study Theology," Vol. 50, 658-661.

15. WA, Vol. 50, 660.

16. I have examined Wesley's prayer life in some detail in my book, *Devotional Life in the Wesleyan Tradition* (Nashville: Upper Room Books, 1983).

17. Wesley's private diaries are housed in e Rylands Library in Manchester, England. His system of noting the "temper" (quality) of his prayers enables us to see when his prayers were moving and meaningful and when they were not.

18. TL, Vol. 4, 490.

19. Frederick Norwood, *Sourcebook of American Methodism* (Nashville: Abingdon Press, 1982), 104-115.

20. Frank Baker, *From Wesley to Asbury* (Durham, NC: Duke University Press, 1976), 188.

21. Terry Teky, *Pray the Price: United Methodists United in Prayer* (Muncie, IN: Prayer Point Press, 1997), 21. This would be an excellent study for you and your small group after you complete this one. It contains biblical, historical, and numerous practical insights to strengthen the personal and corporate prayer life of United Methodists.

22. BW, Vol. 1, 577.

23. If discernment is something new for you or for your church, I would encourage you to read *Discerning God's Will Together* by Danny E. Morris and Charles M. Olson (Nashville: Upper Room Books, 1997).

24. Tekyl, 125-141, Chapter 7, "From Junk Room to Prayer Room."

25. Alvin J. Vander Griend, *The Praying Church Sourcebook* (Grand Rapids, MI: Christian Reformed Church, 1990).

Notes to Chapter 3

1. BW, Vol. 3, 598.

2. JW, Vol. 13, 4.

3. David Wells, *Losing Our Virtue—Why the Church Must Recover Its Moral Vision* (Grand Rapids: Eerdmans, 1998).

4. In one of his earliest published works, *The Character of a Methodist* (1742), he clearly and repeatedly shows that this was his aim in establishing the Methodist movement. And as a means of showing his commitment to classical Christianity, the work itself was based upon the seventh book of the *Stromateis* by Clement of Alexandria (150-215 A.D.).

5. Aelred Burrows OSB, "Wesley the Catholic," in *John Wesley: Contemporary Perspectives* (London: Epworth Press, 1988), 60-61.

6. James Logan, "Wesley and Francis: Two Evangelical Witnesses," *Circuit Rider*, November-December, 1982 (Nashville: United Methodist Publishing House), 5-7.

7. Wesley's first recorded use of the phrase was in his Journal on August 17, 1750 (BW, Vol. 20, 357). He also used it in his sermons *The Late Work of God in North America* (BW, Vol. 3, 598) and *Causes of the Inefficacy of Christianity* (BW, Vol. 4, 90), as well as in letters to William Church on October 13, 1778 (TL, Vol. 6, 324) and to Adam Clarke on January 3, 1787 (TL, Vol. 7, 362).

8. BW, Vol. 9, 69.

9. Dr. Davis Watson has opened the way for contemporary United Methodism to rediscover this central dimension of Wesleyan spirituality. If you have yet to use his resources, I urge you to begin with his book, *Covenant Discipleship* (Nashville: Discipleship Resources, 1989).

10. Greg Clapper, *As if the Heart Mattered* (Nashville, Upper Room Books, 1997), 70-71.

11. Stanley Ayling, *John Wesley* (Nashville: Abingdon Press, 1979), 164.

12. Ted A. Campbell, *John Wesley and Christian Antiquity* (Nashville: Kingswood Books, 1991), 68.

13. John Wesley, *A Christian Library*, 50 vols. (Bristol: Farley, 1749-55). A list of all the authors and works is published in Robert Monk's *John Wesley: His Puritan Heritage* (Nashville: Abingdon Press, 1966), 255-264.

14. JW, Vol. 14, 222-223.

15. Charles W. Ferguson, *Organizing to Beat the Devil* (Garden City, NY: Doubleday, 1971).

16. TL, Vol. 8, 58.

17. John S. Simon, *John Wesley and the Religious Societies* (London: The Epworth Press, 1921).

18. Simon, 19.

19. The custom was to begin biblical exposition at Matthew 1:1 and proceed through the New Testament. This activity created a need for a resource for leaders to use to carry on this work between visits by Wesley or in the absence of other qualified expositors. Wesley responded by publishing *Explanatory Notes Upon the New Testament* in 1755 and *Explanatory Notes Upon the Old Testament* in 1765.

20. JW, Vol. 8, 250.

21. Howard Snyder, *The Radical Wesley* (Grand Rapids: Francis Asbury Press, 1980), 54.

22. Frederick Norwood, *The Story of American Methodism* (Nashville: Abingdon Press, 1974), 131.

23. All the historical references to the sister denominations, leaders, and the Miley quotation are found in Frederick Norwood (ed.), *Sourcebook of American Methodism* (Nashville: Abingdon Press, 1982), 104-105, 109, 169.

Notes to Chapter 4

1. This phrase is used so often in Wesley's writings that it is impossible to cite a single source. One of his most telling uses of it occurred in a letter dated January 10, 1774, and addressed to John Mason, one of the early-Methodist preachers: "If you press all the believers to go on to perfection and to expect deliverance from sin every moment, they will grow in grace. But if ever they lose that expectation, they will grow flat and cold." (TL. Vol. 6, 66).

2. BW. Vol. 2, 91.

3. TL, Vol. 8, 238. This letter was written less than a year before Wesley died. It shows how long and clearly he held to the conviction that God had raised up Methodism to propagate the doctrine of Christian Perfection.

4. Albert Outler, *John Wesley* (New York: Oxford University Press, 1964), 251-305. Dr. Outler gives this extensive treatment in order to document the importance of this idea in our Wesleyan tradition.

5. John G. McEllhenney, ed., *Proclaiming Grace and Freedom: The Story of United Methodism in America* (Nashville: Abingdon Press, 1982), 37.

6. Frederick Norwood, *The Story of American Methodism* (Nashville: Abingdon Press, 1974), 292-297. The picture is further detailed and strengthened by John L. Peters, *Christian Perfection and American Methodism* (Nashville: Pierce and Washabaugh, 1956; reprinted in 1985 by the Francis Asbury Press of Zondervan Publishing House in Grand Rapids, Michigan).

7. David L. McKenna, *Growing Up in Christ* (Indianapolis: Light and Life Communications, 1998), 74.

8. ENT, 368. Commenting on 15:7, Wesley says, "Prayers themselves are a fruit of faith, and they produce more fruit."

9. For additional resources that will help you cultivate this way of prayerfully probing Scripture, see David Thompson, *Bible Study That Works* (Napanee, IN: Evangel Publishing House, 1994) and Robert Traina, *Methodical Bible Study* (Grand Rapids: Zondervan, 1985).

10. E. Stanley Jones, *Growing Spiritually* (Nashville: Abingdon Press, 1953), 293.

11. E. Stanley Jones, *How to be a Transformed Person* (Nashville: Abingdon Press, 1951), 274.

12. *Ibid.*, p. 277.

13. Douglas V. Steere, *Dimensions of Prayer* (Nashville: Upper Room Books, 1997), 80-81.

14. John Dear, ed., *Henri Nouwen: The Road to Peace* (Maryknoll, NY: Orbis Books, 1998), 210.

15. Lucinda Vardey, compiler, *Mother Teresa: A Simple Path* (New York: Ballentine Books, 1995), 35-36.

16. The "Purpose Driven Church Simulcast" is co-sponsored by a number of agencies, including The General Board of Discipleship of The United Methodist Church. For more information about this conference, call (949)-586-2000 or visit the website at www.saddleback.com.